SHINE ON

Irish Writers for Shine

Edited and Introduced
by Pat Boran

Foreword
by Miriam O'Callaghan

DEDALUS PRESS
DUBLIN, IRELAND

ACKNOWLEDGEMENTS

Acknowledgement and grateful thanks are due to all of the writers who generously contributed their work to this anthology; to artist Eamon Colman for permission to include his painting on the cover; to Penguin Ireland for kind permission to include previously published work by Molly McCloskey (from *Circles Around the Sun: In Search of a Lost Brother*, June 2011) and by Leah Mills (*In Your Face*, 2007); to Faber and Faber for permission to reprint 'Dark Horses' by Claire Keegan, originally published in *Walk the Blue Fields* (2007); to Alba Ziegler-Bailey and all at the Wylie Agency (UK) Ltd. for permission to include 'As If There Were Trees' by Colum McCann, copyright © by Colum McCann, all rights reserved; to Nuala Ní Dhomhnaill for permission to include her poem 'An Bhatráil' and to Paul Muldoon for permission to include his translation, 'The Battering', both of which previously appeared in *The Wake Forest Book of Irish Women's Poetry, 1967–2000*, ed. Peggy O'Brien; to Gabriel Rosenstock for permission to include his translations of poems by Liam Ó Muirthile; to Micheál Ó hAodha for his English language translation, and to Cló Iar-Chonnachta, the original publishers of Gabriel Rosenstock's travelogue, *Ólann mo Mhiúil as an nGainséis;* to the Gallery Press for permission to reprint John Montague's 'A Holy Vision', from *Speech Lessons* (2011); to Salmon Poetry for permission to reprint Jessie Lendennie's 'Midnight' from *Daughter and Other Poems* (2002) and 'Grattan Road' from *Waking Here* (2011). The following are from a number of recent Dedalus Press publications: 'In the End' by Paul Murray is taken from *These Black Stars* (2003); 'A Mother Mourns Her Heroin-Addicted Daughter' by Leland Bardwell is from *The Noise of Masonry Settling* (2006); 'Bill' by Pádraig J Daly is from *The Voice of the Hare* (1997); 'Black Dogs' by Paddy Bushe is from 'To Ring in Silence: New and Selected Poems' (2008); and 'To the Book of Kells' by Paul Perry is from *The Last Falcon and Small Ordinance* (2010). 'Advice for Writers' by Pat Boran was first broadcast on *Sunday Miscellany*, RTÉ Radio 1.

COMHAIRLE CHONTAE ÁTHA CLIATH THEAS
SOUTH DUBLIN COUNTY LIBRARIES

CASTLETYMON BRANCH LIBRARY
TO RENEW ANY ITEM TEL: 452 4888
OR ONLINE AT www.southdublinlibraries.ie

Items should be returned on or before the last date below. Fines, as displayed in the Library, will be charged on overdue items.

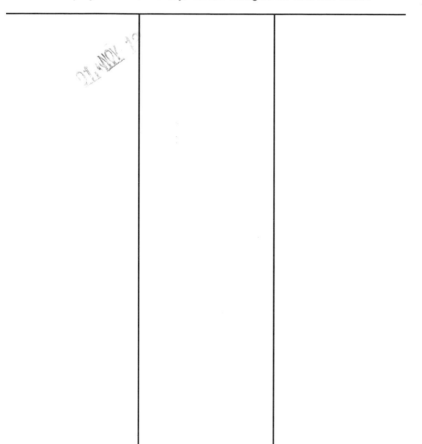

First published in 2011 by
The Dedalus Press
13 Moyclare Road
Baldoyle
Dublin 13
Ireland

www.dedaluspress.com

ISBN 978 1 906614 46 1 paperback
ISBN 978 1 906614 47 8 hardbound

Dedalus Press titles are represented in the UK by
Central Books, 99 Wallis Road, London E9 5LN
and in North America by Syracuse University Press, Inc.,
621 Skytop Road, Suite 110, Syracuse, New York 13244.

The cover image is a detail from 'In the Land of the Grandfather Trees'
by Eamon Colman, reproduced here by kind permission of the artist.
www.eamoncolman.com

The Dedalus Press receives financial assistance from
The Arts Council / An Chomhairle Ealaíon

CONTENTS

FOREWORD

by Miriam O'Callaghan

I T IS A PLEASURE to write the foreword for this book. I am a great supporter of the work of Shine and I have been involved with previous projects of Shine's, including the launch of the See Change Campaign and the 'Taking Control of Your Mental Health' magazine a couple of years ago.

In these challenging times people are undergoing a lot of stress in their lives which can lead to mental health problems. I believe that everyone should be aware of and take care of their own mental health, just as we do with our physical health.

Creative writing can be one of the useful diversions from the stress we encounter in our everyday lives, whether you like to write yourself or take pleasure in reading other authors' work. I was very impressed by the large number of well-known writers who have made meaningful contributions to this publication. The fact that so many writers have submitted pieces shows that they also believe in Shine and that mental health issues should be written about willingly. This book is a wonderful opportunity to raise awareness about a topic that is not often discussed openly and to break the silence surrounding mental health problems.

One in four of us will experience a mental health problem at some point in our life. Even if you're not affected directly, you probably know someone – a friend, a family member or a colleague – who has been affected by mental ill health.

The reason I got involved with this project is because I believe in the valuable work carried out by Shine. The primary purpose of this book is to raise awareness about mental health and to promote the valuable services Shine offers to people with mental health problems as well as their family members and carers.

Everyone deserves the same opportunities in life, and it is time to break down the stigma associated with mental health problems and allow each one of us to be open and honest about our own personal experiences.

I hope you enjoy reading the wonderful short stories and poetry in this book.

Best wishes,

Miriam O'Callaghan

INTRODUCTION

I struck the board and cry'd, No more.
I will abroad.
— George Herbert, 'The Collar'

G EORGE HERBERT'S BEST-KNOWN POEM 'The Collar' —
which many of us will remember from school — begins
with something of a jolt, a violent blow, an angry, frustrated
voice addressing God. 'What?' he says, 'shall I ever sigh and pine?'
Do you think I'm just going to sit here and suffer this?

It's more than three decades since I first encountered 'The
Collar' and imagined Herbert, an Anglican clergyman, bringing
his fist down in anger on his writing desk (and sending up a fog of
chalk dust, as I envisioned it in the CBS, Tower Hill, Portlaoise).
Even then the poem seemed extraordinary for the sheer charge, the
sound and the fury unleashed in its opening lines. My classmates
and I may not have loved it as much as we did the stripped-back
nightmare blues of Emily Dickinson's 'Because I could not stop
for Death' (more given, as we were, to minor vices than to major
verse), but none of us could fail to be impressed by the emotional
outburst, the force of Herbert's passion.

If anything, it put me in mind of Peter Finch's portrayal of the
distressed newscaster Howard Beale in the 1970s movie *Network*,
where he challenges his viewers to go to their windows and shout
out into the American night, 'I'm mad as hell and I'm not to going
to take it any more.'

At the end of the poem, Herbert finds that his rebellion against
the constraints of his vocation are short-lived. But it doesn't take
from a poem in which the internal struggle of one man is not
simply reported in summary but played out live before the reader,

a personal even private drama in which the reader is intimately involved.

Since my schooldays I've returned many times to 'The Collar', not least for its tacit suggestion that strain, struggle, distress and even anger might all be triggers and even fitting subject matter for poems. The poem serves as a reminder that poetry, and creative writing of all kinds, need not be restricted to a rosy, greeting card vision of the world. If the *Soundings* anthology had a number of serious failings – a startling gender imbalance, a suggestion that, with few exceptions, poetry was something that had happened in the historical past – even so it included a remarkable range of tones and registers, from the confiding to the confrontational, the contemplative to the deeply conflicted – had we only the ears and life experience at 16 years of age to hear them. Good writing, the book tried to show us, whatever else it was, was the result of pressures of thought and feeling, contained (and sometimes only just) by the formal abilities of its authors. It derived, in one way or another, from altered states. Everything is the same for days on end and then, one day, something changes: it is from that change that the poem or story derives its energy.

In some ways this no-doubt routine discovery made poetry and literature not just relevant for me but raised it to the level of a sustaining passion. If poems and other literary forms are reports back from a variety of altered states, the value of those reports will depend on the writer's ability to observe and describe, to locate his or her sensations in a precisely rendered external world. As readers, we can enter internal experience – Herbert's anger, Wordsworth's heartbreak at the loss of a child, Dickinson's chill vision, or Kavanagh's sense of rapture with simply being still alive – through the external details the writers provide.

The notion of altered states I've found to be hugely valuable when discussing with others the creative process, the journey that creative acts involve. In classrooms or writing workshops, for instance, it immediately dispels the notion that writing is a passive activity. It reminds us that writing is, at once, about the world as well as about the self. And by so doing, it helps the writer exploring personal issues to connect to the world, and the writer focusing on the observable world to earth those observations in lived, felt experience.

One has to be careful, of course, not to force creative writing into some dramatic cul de sac, all histrionics and no substance. The stereotype of creative individuals, for instance, often involves a dramatically altered state and succeeds only in distancing them from our own everyday experience, in making them less human. Think of how we reduce Einstein to the disheveled 'nutty professor' beloved of admen, or the genius of Van Gogh to a caricature of the 'mad' artist cutting off his own ear, as if work and focus and the struggle to contain and communicate were not also a huge part of the work of both. Like most stereotypes, these do more to obscure than to reveal.

In truth, far from being the preserve of some elite, many of us will remember – and recognise when we encounter them again – the altered states that result from falling in or out of love, from bereavement, childbirth, joyous good luck or crushing defeat, and a whole range of other 'symptoms' the passing of time had yet to alleviate. Our CVs record who we are, what we did and when, but our diaries and our art – our poems and songs and stories perhaps especially – record what happened to us along the way, the changes we made, the changes we suffered. They depict us off-balance, out-of-kilter, at a loss; *Nel mezzo del cammin di nostra vita,* in the middle of our life's path, as Dante begins his *Inferno*, having left one certainty and perhaps with 'miles to go' before the next.

2.

According to a study by psychologist Kay Redfield Jamison, reported on *BBC News* in February 2011, 'The incidence of mood disorders, suicide and institutionalisation was 20 times higher among major British and Irish poets between 1600 and 1800 … In other words, poets are 20 times more likely to end up in an asylum than the general population.'

Whether psychiatric disturbance follows on from the writing of poetry, or vice versa, is a moot point and certainly one that is beyond the scope of a volume like this. One might argue, of course, that the intensely personal, often autobiographical, and occasionally confessional nature of literary writing in general may significantly affect a writer's relationship with his or her society – though equally it has been argued that the challenged mind will often turn to writing or art in order to try to make sense of internal experience, to view it, as it were, at arm's-length. Either way, the individual who commits a traumatic experience to words is unlikely to be freed of it or 'healed' by it (as some alarmingly simplistic theses might suggest), though the struggle to manipulate details, to match subject with form, may be a useful first step towards finding a new perspective.

Even so, the purpose of this book, and of the contributions gathered here, is not therapeutic. Though arguably of a different kind and scale, the altered states with which I began this introduction are to some extent known to us all, but perhaps particularly to those of us who attempt to put down in words what would otherwise be transitory ideas, vague voices, suspicions and hints of meaning for ourselves and for all to see. 'Hell talkt my brain awake,' John Berryman wrote in *77 Dream Songs*. 'Bluffed to the ends of me pain / & I took up a pencil.' Whether or not there is a direct correspondence between mental health and writing, I believe it will be clear from this book that a real and meaningful empathy exists among the writing community for those afflicted by mental ill health, perhaps because creative writing, whatever else it might be, is so often a controlled experiment in the limits and extent of the self.

3.

It is unlikely that anyone has picked up this book to read an unqualified amateur like myself attempt an overview of mental ill health and its possible connections to creative writing. And yet no editor could produce an anthology such as this without beginning to wonder about that relationship, and without going on to notice the thread-like links between the two emerging in the text.

'[W]hen you reached out to love, / all you could see were lips move / in silence,' writes Philip Casey in a poem entitled 'Cruelty', turning the volume down on the world and forcing our emotional selves, our altered selves perhaps, to cross the gap by lip-reading, by making an imaginative leap towards meaning.

That sense of an enforced silence is one of the most striking aspects of those poems and stories which deal with the way in which mental ill health is experienced by friends and family. Tony Curtis, for instance, writing about the American poet Elizabeth Bishop (whose mother spent the last 18 years of her life in an asylum) echoes the form of Bishop's own 'Visits to St. Elizabeth's', itself a grim echo of the childhood favourite 'The House That Jack Built':

> These are the years of electro-shock therapy.
> There are sparks in her ears,
> there is a gag in her mouth.
> She rarely screams now,
> only in dreams.

Communication is strained or impossible, prohibited. The world denies the sufferer the right of expression.

Inevitably, many of the writers offer work that commemorates friends and acquaintances, family members and neighbours who took their own lives. The contributions, though typically gentle and careful, are charged with that urge to break the silence. The grim statistics of suicide and self-harm in our country speak for themselves, but the memory of a time when the subject could not be discussed haunts many of us and an entire volume might have been made of only those poems and stories which attempt to bring this dark fact into the light.

As he has done so brilliantly and courageously for decades, in 'Thinking About Suicide' Paul Durcan writes unflinchingly about loneliness and despair, his own and that of others, such as the woman he meets on the street

> Who rocks back on her heels in her pink, hooped skirt
> With laughter, no matter what the topic.

As ever, the best writing is that which risks the exposure of the self even as it confronts the world around it. Molly McCloskey, for instance, writes of a sibling's early signs of schizophrenia: 'By the following year I am old enough to be embarrassed by his oddness, to want to distance myself from whatever is wrong with him,' the clear lens of her prose recording in two directions at once. Christine Dwyer Hickey, meanwhile, in 'The Aviary' explores wider familial relationships through a fictional narrative where a mother's declaration about her visiting niece – 'I just wish Giovanna didn't speak her mind quite so much' – seems to register not just the family's but the reader's own growing unease.

Others of the contributors record the seemingly out-of-nowhere arrival of unexpected behavior or moods, a sudden unexplained turn or outright overthrowing of a norm, though we quickly see that, in general, it is the nature of storytelling itself, its narrative framing and jump-cuts, that creates the sense of sudden change. In retrospect, at least, we often srealise that trouble was brewing long before it finally arrived.

'Rose Wynne went mad / One summer's morning, / Stripped off her clothes, / Right down to her skin,' begins Vincent Woods' poem 'Madness', while Theo Dorgan, among others, looking back sees hints of what was to come for a school friend: 'Never had much to say for himself, Jimmy. / Teachers walked carefully around him, sensing the edge / on that considered silence …' Faced with unexplained changes in behaviour, with dark and troubling turns, those of us blessed by exclusion become at best amateur sleuths, forced to try to piece together the clues.

4.

The idea of producing this anthology came from John Saunders, the Director of Shine, who wondered if a volume of writing in support of the voluntary body might help to raise awareness of its work at a challenging time. The proposal seemed to me a real opportunity to make a meaningful contribution.

While figuring out the modus operandi for the book (it's not everyday that a voluntary body and a small literary publisher join forces), John and I were immediately in agreement that, whatever publication would result, it should not be an anthology limited to writing about mental ill health, *per se,* but a general and diverse collection of contemporary prose and poetry, including work related to the aim of the book but refusing to present the subject of mental ill health as separate from the many issues that matter to us as a society.

In inviting contributions, therefore, I welcomed whatever kind of work the writers felt able to offer in the moment – glimpses, as it were, of their creative process at the time. The support and solidarity of the writers, I suggested in my letter of invitation, might be the most meaningful contribution they could make.

The sense of there being a community of writers, across genres and formal approaches, is one that is not often enough recognised or celebrated. Writing is a solitary activity, and yet, given an opportunity to stand together, all of these individual writers grasped the opportunity to act as part of a group, part of a guild, one might almost say, with all of that word's connotations of individual pursuit and talent, motivation and ambition, but common purpose. The writers gathered herein, and the artist Eamon Colman who gave us permission to use his work on the cover, contributed to this anthology freely and free of charge, immediately and without fuss, eager to lend their support even when they had yet to face the page or screen to see what they might be able to come up with, what might come up for them.

Others too were invited to contribute, but it is in the nature of the writing life that one cannot always respond to external requests or invitations. And it should be said that those who declined did so with apologies, keen to stress that, had circumstances (or the muse) been otherwise inclined, they should have been happy to contribute. A small number, constrained by work-in-progress or looming deadlines, yet keen to participate, offered something from a previously published work. And, though I had started out looking for previously uncollected material, ever happy to break my own rules for a cause, I gladly accepted.

So it was that the initial idea took on this present form. I should say at this point that there are many other excellent writers whom I did not have the opportunity to approach, simply because the book, having so quickly taken on a life of its own, had to be kept to a manageable size.

Whether the altered states of mental ill health and creative expression have anything substantial in common, or whether the practice of the latter can have an ameliorating effect on the former, *Shine On* is, I think, an extraordinary statement of belief in the value of writing and its importance in and to our society. An expression of hope as well as of concern, it will, I trust, find its own way in the world, a small addition to the bright beacon that Shine, through its various activities, holds up over the troubled waters of so many lives.

– Pat Boran

ALEX BARCLAY

I Have Only Ever Loved

OUR FIRST DATE was in the old bar with the painted wallpaper, and the smell of smoke. At last orders, you answered the call of the bell. I smiled at the girl on the table beside me with her thumbs up. We had the blessing of a stranger. But when half an hour passed, and I spent it alone, I thought you were gone ... until you appeared with two drinks in each hand.

On our first holiday, we had a row at dinner. I stormed away from words I can't even remember. I walked strange, winding streets, past tables of laughter and love, and through tears I could see the kind of family I wanted us to become. It is better to have loved and lost, I thought. The hotel room was empty when I got back. You had put your suitcase in the wardrobe. I sat on the bed, barely able to breathe. I thought you were gone ... until I heard the sound of your key.

Another time, with another key, I let myself into your apartment, and I found you crying. You told me how unhappy you were, and how you were not the man for me, and that you should never have proposed, and as I looked into your heartbreaking face, I thought you were gone ... until you looked into mine.

Our wedding day was filled with everything we were, and everyone we loved. But if I had walked down the aisle and found you at the end, curled in a ball, weeping, I would have picked you up and taken you wherever you needed to be. No white dress or flowers, no three courses or two signatures or first dance would have broken my stride.

So, as you lie in our bed and you can't make the shower, you are loved. When the lights are off, and the door is shut, and your work is not done, and my lips are unkissed, you are loved. With your unwashed hair, and your hollow cheeks, and your round-the-clock shadow, and eyes as sad as I've ever seen, you are no less than the beautiful man you were on the night we met, or married.

You are not terrible, or a burden. I did not make a mistake. You are not pathetic, or ugly, you are not useless or weak. I am not disgusted or repelled. I am not deserted, or alone.

Last night, with your back turned to me, you said:

'I'm gone. I think I'm gone.'

I wrapped my arms around you, pressed my head against your shoulder. I felt your stubble, and your heart, I heard your breath, I smelled your skin. I saw how your wedding ring slips to your knuckle when your hand hangs limp.

Still, you light all my senses. So, wherever you think you are, you are not gone.

You were never gone.

I have never loved and lost. I have only ever loved.

LELAND BARDWELL

A Mother Mourns Her Heroin-Addicted Daughter

How could I have dreamt
That my bird of paradise,
My green-clad hippie girl,
Could be so reduced
To the gammon face of poverty,
The incessant whinge of a child.

If we rolled up time like a ball
I'd give you the cherries of my nipples,
I'd wash you almond clean
And lay your hair like lint
On the cartilage of my breast.

A prey to the barren street, you're lost
On the breach of years that no silk
Nor cotton drawing-to of threads
Can mend. The void. Your path is marked
Like gull-prints on an empty beach.

The drug has perished your will.
You float like a stick on a pond
In here, in there – to a harbour of lily-trees,
Or held for days in scum till the light
Breeze lifts you and you edge along.

Will you walk on my street once more?
I'll raise my pavements to keep you safe,
Open the balcony of my arms.
I will buckle your shoes again
And shine the mirror for your dance.

But you will not throw away your bag of tricks.
Your monkey fingers cling to the safety net
In which you nightly land, having walked
The trembling wire and heard the screams
Of anticipation, seen the up-turned mouths.

How can we meet down the glaciers
Of days, the furnaces of nights?

KEVIN BARRY

Decimator

THAT WAS THE SUMMER I took messages from the birdsong and sprayed my name in silver along the box hedge of Mr Sweeney's side garden

DECIMATOR

That was the summer I lay in the woods on the edge of town past the football fields and on the ground before me I spelled out with sticks and fallen branches the single word

DECIMATOR

That was the summer I lived on the top floor of the multi-storey car-park and I looked down over the blur of the night traffic and the lights of the cars made a pattern across the streets from the cold syllables of

DECIMATOR

I was seventeen. I felt as if I was filmed at every moment of the day and night. I was living on cold meats and fags. I was a runt for seventeen. I wore pancake foundation and a thick circling of eyeliner. I lived on the top-floor landing of an emergency stairwell beside the elevator shaft at the multi-storey. The landing was about eight foot by four, and shaded from the strip lights. It had a high, oblong window that from my tiptoes gave a view across to an apartment building. I told time by church bells and each night, just past midnight, an old couple slow-danced to a crackly old record in an apartment over there. He wore a cardigan and slacks and she wore a slip. 'Falling In Love Again,' the chorus went, but it was ancient and sung in a foreign accent, and it travelled across the crevice of the street:

'Fallink in't lahf again …'

The old couple were so smug and I aimed for them and mimed a trigger pull, and I plugged in my headphones against their song. I had a sleeping bag up there on the stairwell. I had a double-cassette recorder. I made compilation tapes for the girls who worked in the goth boutique. I wrote them no tracklists, I wrote nothing at all on the inlay cards except for one word

DECIMATOR

and it wasn't as if they were crawling out of their fishnet bodices in gratitude but I had kissed one of them, Angie, smack on her blue lipstick, and it felt like stepping off a rooftop and not falling but ascending.

I met her in town the next day and she blanked me. I said hello and she looked scared and she bolted for the coffee shop. She left me standing on the side of O'Connell Street. I stared at the cracks in the pavement, the maplines of them leading who knows where. I walked away in the opposite direction, and the camera swivelled to follow me. I felt a blush come up, and a spike of nausea in my throat. I followed my army boots along, and it was a Saturday, the town was busy, and every face I passed had a kind of summery, easy-going look to it, as if the world mightn't spin from its axis at any given moment.

I went down to the river and crawled under the bridge and I hung off the girders for a while.

My father kept a shotgun though years had passed since he'd gone out the quarry to shoot any rabbits.

Lampin', he used to call it. He used to go in a sawn-off Volkswagon Beetle, Saturday nights into Sunday mornings, and he'd shoot all night, but my father did none of the things he used to do. He didn't fish or shoot or drink or put the hard word on women. He just sat around the house, feeding guilt into himself like he was picking at a basket of plums, and he stared into the grate of the fireplace. He'd rotate one thumb slowly around the other, and I knew I was as well to be out of there.

Underneath the bridge, I imagined the feeling of the gun in my hands. I listened as the traffic creased along overhead, leaving town – the *shlank, shlanking* of its movement on the metal bridge – and I drifted awhile on the rhythms of it.

The hot day wilted and evening came up off the river. When dusk settled, about ten o'clock, I walked out along the river, and I came on the dock road that would bring me home – to the home I didn't use anymore – to where the shotgun was kept.

I hadn't been back since the incident with Mr Sweeney's box hedge. The letters I sprayed in silver to spell out the word

DECIMATOR

were written a foot tall, and it was a rotten piece of vandalism, in all fairness, because Mr Sweeney in fact was a lovely man, and he kept a very nice box hedge. I felt really terrible about it. It was if I wasn't cut out to be a juvenile delinquent at all. But I had not been in full control of my faculties. I had drank cider and brandy that night, and I had gone at the anti-histamine inhalers, again, and also cough bottle, and a full can of Studio Line hairspray that I sniffed from a plastic bag. I think it was the hairspray that tipped me over the edge. The worst of it was the Sweeneys were our next-door neighbours, and it wasn't as if I was going to get away with it, coz everybody on the estate knew that I tagged myself

DECIMATOR

and anyway a squad car pulled up, the guards caught me in the act. It was four in the morning, just as I put the final curl on the

R in Decimator, and it didn't help that I was bollock naked at the time and had a ferocious nosebleed in full flow.

The look they gave me.

My father was woken by the guards and he came out of the house. He stood there in his shorts, by the front door, his jaw lolling, half asleep, half wretched. I reeled around the front garden, legless, nude, bleeding. My father just shook his great fat head and said:

'You can sling your fuckin' hook altogether now, boy, y'hear me?'

The guards made him fetch pants for me. They took me away in the squad car. They took me down the station and threw me into a cell until I was good and hungover in the hard bright ache of morning. They left me out to the streets with promise of a summons, and there was nothing for it but to move into the multi-storey.

But that was four days back, and plenty had happened since. Things were moving quick.

As I headed for my old home, the dock road was sketchy and dangerous-feeling. The hoors roamed and the kerb-crawlers eased up and rolled their windows for them. I felt nauseous but I walked through it all with my head down. I followed the lines of the telephone wires along the dock road. I skulked out of town as the blackbirds sang a taunt at me.

Our estate was on the far edge of the town. The houses were built on what used to be swamp. As I came on the estate, there was still light in the sky but everything was in blue shadow, the houses were dark outlines, the shouts of children floated by, and I came to our house, number 124, and I shinned over the side gate. In the back garden, I followed each breath along towards the shed. I tried not to look in the house. I tried not to turn or make sudden movements that might alert him, but I couldn't resist. I saw him in the back room, what used to be the dining room. He'd fetched the television in there, and I was mesmerized by the sight of him;

I might have stood there forever. I saw every tendril of sorrow that rose from him, each a wisp of thin white smoke, and each tangled again as it climbed, and he was suspended from a great floating weight of sorrow above. I imagined it as a kind of airship.

After my first night in the multi-storey – a sleepless night – I had drifted into the woods, on a very bright day, when the sun's assault was livid and constant, and I wanted the green reprieve of the woods, the dapple and cool of it. We'd had a wet spring and the earth floor of the woods had some give and squelch in it still. I found just the place, and I spelt out with sticks and branches on the needly floor of the wood the word

DECIMATOR

and I wept until I was sore. I could find no bearings at all. I stayed there until night. I filled a plastic bag with hairspray and breathed in deeply from it and I felt my heart expand to its pulsing red limits. My head was scrunched violently back to my shoulder blades by a great force of loathing and what I saw above me then was the pale, pocked face of the moon come through a gap in the summer canopy, and I closed my eyes and settled into the paleness.

I drifted awhile on the rivers of the moon. I lay buried there for the slow arc of the night. Small animals rustled and the night birds sang. The words that they sang were for her, and described her in the tiniest detail – I saw her exquisitely, her hands on her hips, sardonic in a doorway, shaded against the light behind her, a darkness against the light, mother-shaped – and the words that the birds sang would never bring her back.

The light began to bleed through around four, and I shivered hard in the damp, cool earth, and just when I thought I could take no more I felt the weirdest thing, a sensation of lightness disguised as hunger. I discovered I was starving with the hunger, and I knew that hunger can only be a want for life. I stomped on my daft boots back out of the woods again.

At the Esso station I bought a packet of corned beef, and I ate all the slices, one after the other; it tasted like angel food.

Twelve hours later I was stone cold in love.

I met Angie underneath the bridge. I knew her from the goth boutique where she worked Saturdays but it was the first time I had properly talked to her. She was a runt, too – about four feet ten, I'd say, technically a dwarf – but she was perfect, beautiful, with a sly upturn to her nose, and a lip-ring, and she was hopelessly posh. We were together in a group beneath the bridge, drinking, but we were alone, too. I told her I had wanted to bury myself to the neck outside in the woods the night before and she looked properly impressed. We watched a spider work a web across the bridge's rusted girders, and we were awed by its measured, shelving descent of the web strands. I told Angie I lived now at the multistorey and about the old couple who slow-danced at midnight and the crackly record they played. I sang a bar of it for fun:

'Fahlink in lahf again …'

She told me it was by Marlene Dietrich and was from a film called *The Blue Angel*.

'That's delicious,' I said. 'Blue Angel.'

We went to the Bat Cave nightclub later. She had free passes. I drowned in the blue-and-mauve sparkling of her eyeshadow. We danced. The lighting effects were one-dimensional and of no danger to epileptics. We danced for a while – Angie all po-faced and blue-lipsticked, me all pale and sexily depressed – and at last on the black fur seats down the back of the club, she leaned in to me, and I kissed her but not for long.

From the shadows of the back garden I watched my father. We had been never been able to talk to each other. There was too great a difference in our ages, he had been in his forties already when I was born, and since my mother died off we had not talked at all. I was pain to him because I was a reminder of her. Her end was quick, with no warning, and there was no time for the words that should be spoken, that even I could have spoken.

I went to the shed and fetched from its hiding place the shotgun. I opened it and checked and saw that it held a single shell. As I came out again through the garden, with the shotgun under my arm, I tried a practice aim at my father but he did not turn to see me.

Along the dock road I went, with the shotgun hidden beneath my army coat, and the river surged blackly as I walked counter to it, and it had news for me, unquestionably.

I ascended in the lift at the multi-storey. I went to my landing and crouched awhile on my haunches. I laid out the shotgun along the sleeping bag, and I slowed my breath as best as I could. The multi-storey was so quiet at night, its great drifts of hollow and echo, and the traffic on the streets far below was thin and indifferent to me. I knew the instant before the church bells sounded they were about to strike midnight. It was as though inside I had been keeping track of time. I stood on tiptoe, with the shotgun, by the high oblong window, and yes they danced over there, him in his cardigan, and her in her slip:

'Falliiink' in lahf again …'

I tried to settle an aim on them but I was unsteady on my tiptoes. I thought if I stood on the cassette recorder, I'd have the extra foot I needed for a true shot. I reached for it then and found in one of the cassette decks a piece of paper. It was folded over and there was a single word written on it and though I had never seen her writing before I recognised it at once as Angie's hand. I read it aloud

DECIMATOR

and I unfolded the piece of paper and it was a free pass for the Bat Cave, for the next night. She had come back for me. I carefully removed the live shell from the shotgun. I hid the shotgun inside the sleeping bag. I was seventeen and I was living on fags and cold meats in a multi-storey car-park. In the distance the river surged through its province of darkness, and life was as sweet as could be.

The blue lipstick was Angie's, and the sparkling of her eyeshadow, and the streak of coppertone she wore that summer in her hair. These were the colours of a rescue.

SARA BERKELEY

Fall Back

November again. Isn't this one
always coming around, with its
dead letter days, its footfalls
on wet leaves, its numbed sounds?

There'll be no more laughter now,
and not a lot of happy ever after.
My mother is missing. The stars too,
the stars are not where I left them,
they are not in their constellations.

Through the keyhole of midnight
I have glimpsed the white tiles
of the future, the stark walls
and the uncut shadows. Losing her
to her own life is one thing –

now and then we all take on water,
sink a little lower – but this little
understood, misdiagnosed, neurological
disaster: that this should have
my mother now just seems unsound.

But there it is: the tug of war
between antagonistic muscle groups,
the lost inhibition of wayward
neurons. *Paralysis agitans*. Eventually,
I am told, every movement

must be voluntarily controlled. Today
our creek is suddenly running wild,
following the season's first storm;
walnut leaves, black locust clog the drain
until our road's awash with rain;

the wind soughs in the thickening black,
last night, we fell back, and the clocks
with their one frail extra hour
snatched us out of the jaws of the dark.

DERMOT BOLGER

Maggie

WHEN I LOOK BACK at the early 1980s now, it is not people's faces that I recall so much. Not those bedsits in Ranelagh and Rathmines with cheap plywood wardrobes, the rotten window-frames installed by slave labour during the famine, the electricity meters with their insatiable fetish for fifty-pence pieces, the French impressionistic posters behind which girls tried to hide damp stains on their walls, or the landlords, who always seemed to be Garda sergeants still wearing their uniform trousers when collecting rent on Thursday nights.

I remember all that and the gap-toothed derelict sites where multi-storey offices now stand, but which leant Dublin the resemblance of a city that had endured a silent blitz. But what I remember most of all, what is crystallised among my most scared memories, is a girl's tiny bedsit on Oratorio Terrace, overlooking the Grand Canal, and how her life seemed mapped out on the worn soles of her black shoes.

I met Maggie in the International Bar two weeks before Christmas in 1983, back when dinosaurs and dodos roamed the back lanes of Donnybrook and T-Rex rode high in the charts. She was part of a boisterous Christmas office party, yet not part of it at all. The others were permanent staff and she was a temporary typist, filling in for someone. I got talking to her and when we slipped away I noticed that nobody else noticed that she had put her coat on. We tried to find somewhere quiet to drink, but there were Christmas parties everywhere, spilling out onto the streets. So in the end we just sat on in the cold on some steps and talked.

We were still talking at half-eleven, when the usual mad scramble occurred for the last bus as hordes emerged from pubs like scrambled RAF crews. I remember thick cigarette smoke on the upper deck of the 16A, the lights of Christmas decorations flashing on and off in shop windows as the bus lumbered up George's Street and Wexford Street. Although I had always regarded them as tacky, that night the decorations seemed magical because I was staring out at them while seated next to Maggie.

All evening I'd been moaning about my job in an insurance office, about the monotony of filing and long coffee breaks. But Maggie made me realise how lucky I was as she described trying to survive on scraps of temporary work, moving from office to office, filling in for people out sick, always being let go in a city with no work, ever since homesickness drew her back from London. She was from Limerick and twenty-two years old – two years younger than me.

I got off the bus at her stop, but did not expect to get asked in. We kissed, standing on the wooden gates over the canal lock as groups of revellers passed, leaving Christmas office parties. When she took my hand I thought it was to say goodnight, but instead she led me past bicycles chained to the banisters in the hallway, up to her bedsit. There were a few clothes on a rail, some mismatched bowls and plates and a tiny crib she had purchased somewhere. I opened a bottle of Blue Nun she had been saving and we drank from cracked cups.

'This place is poky,' Maggie said, 'but at least it's mine, though it wasn't easy to save up the deposit. It beats London. London is lonely but I didn't want to go back to Limerick. I suppose Dublin is a half way house – it's not home, but not over there.'

'Where will you spend Christmas?' I asked.

'Here. There's nothing for me in Limerick anymore.'

'That will be lonely. A beautiful young woman, all alone.'

She shrugged, embarrassed. 'Don't be daft, there's nothing beautiful about me. I'm as ordinary as they come.'

'There's something beautiful about you.'

'What?'

Maggie had kicked off her shoes and I bent down to pick one

up. Warm inside and slightly moist. She watched me run my fingers over it.

'What are you doing, Michael?'

I wasn't sure how to reply. How do you tell a girl that what you noticed first was her feet and what you really fell for were her black shoes and how her life seemed mapped out on the scuffed soles. Some men worship shoes, elaborate stilettos with phallic heels designed more for foreplay than roadways. That kink never interested me but now I was discovering a curiosity inside me that needed curing. How could I explain this desire to her that made no sense to myself? But four years of surviving on her own meant that, although Maggie still possessed a strange innocence, I sensed that nothing would shock her anymore.

'It's your shoes,' I said.

'What about them? Are they dirty? I'm sorry.'

'No. They're beautiful.'

Maggie laughed, a little nervously, and took back her shoe.

'You're cracked, Michael. Those shoes are ancient, all I can afford.'

'They're beautiful because they belong to you. You're beautiful and just don't realise it.'

'Stop being daft.'

'Do you want me to go home, Maggie, or do you want me to stay?'

'I want to wake up beside you, because I'm so tired of waking up on my own.'

'Then, can I ask you to do something, Maggie?'

Her eyes were serious. I wondered what other men had asked.

'Tonight, when we ... could you leave your shoes on?'

Maggie looked at the shoe in her hand. When she looked up her eyes were without guile. 'When you're lonely you're vulnerable, Michael, and trust me, when you're vulnerable men ask you to do far worse things than that.'

We undressed with the light out. When she knelt on her bed

in the moonlight I could see out through the lace curtains into other bedsits in the extension next door. Squares of wallpaper, a loaf of bread on a table. All those isolated lives. Below Maggie's body I saw the scuffed soles of her shoes, repeatedly re-heeled and repaired. They faced towards me, exposed. The miles she had walked in them, from temporary job to temporary job, The stairs she had climbed seeking a small flat to call her own. The times they had been patched up as she struggled to save enough for a deposit on her dreams. Those shoes seemed to offer me her life story, saying this is what I really am, neither ashamed nor proud. I felt such tenderness, felt that we would never be more naked that at that moment with just her shoes between us. And I knew I loved her, if I only had the courage to say so. I loved her grit and courage as she traipsed from interview to interview, making friends and making do without ever losing hope or a sense of loneliness. She trembled slightly and I knew she felt exposed, not by her nakedness but in a way she could not understand, as if she sensed that somehow I was glimpsing her soul in a fashion that would never occur again. Afterwards, when I lay curled against her back, she asked could she take them off.

'Yes,' I said. 'I've seen all I'll ever need to see.'

I wish I knew what happened to Maggie. We never quarrelled, but ... I don't know ... maybe that first night was so intimate that afterwards nothing could ever be as intense again. In January she lost her job, fell behind with her rent, found her possessions in two plastic sacks outside the front door. She wouldn't take help, gave me a new address but when I went looking she wasn't there. She owns a part of me still.

I have three children now, a detached house in Dalkey that we bought before the property boom, an apartment in the Czech Republic managed by a letting agency, a company car, a brilliant pension fund. The sort of security that Maggie and I used to dream about, curled up together in her single bed. Yet I think we never really believed in the absurd notion that one day we would become middle-aged. I only ever saw Maggie once again, a year later. It was Christmas time again, festive shoppers rushing about. She was queueing for a bus in O'Connell Street, wearing the same coat and same shoes.

She claimed to have a boyfriend, a new job, a nice flat, but I didn't believe her. I had just cashed my pay cheque, the landlord waiting for his cut. I decided to dodge him and led Maggie into Clarks shoe-shop to pick a comfortable pair of new shoes, a Christmas present, I said. She kept protesting but she was touched by the gesture and touched too when I asked if I might keep her old pair. I have them still, hidden away in the attic in an old bag of golf gear that my wife is always suggesting I throw out. I've haven't touched them in twenty years. I just like to know that her shoes are still there, my secret code, proof that I was knelt on a single bed one Christmas with the girl who wore them, with nothing else between us except an undeclared love.

PAT BORAN

Advice for Writers

Write what you know
or write what you don't.
Or write what you don't know you know – you know? –
what you can't, what you won't...

Write what seems too trivial, too dense, too dark;
write as if every drop of ink were a bright spark.

The scarecrows of childhood, teenage nightmares,
midlife's apparitions and vague fears.
Write about these. What you half understand,
never forgot, won't ignore, can't outrun,
not if you run for a year.

Write what you spy with your little eye
but have never studied before.
With your heart on your sleeve,
with your gut in a knot,
with the bailiffs outside banging on your door.

The candlelight procession that is rush-hour,
the devotional gaze of the commuters,
and, in the car-park behind the railway station,
the sacred altar of the burnt-out car.

Sleep as much as possible, then not for days.
Drink for Ireland, but give your friends the slip;
skip Main Street and head for the edge of town,
the ghosts estates patrolled by dogs, and men

dreaming of their lovers, the liminal zones;
risk disturbing the 'better-left-alone'.

Mushrooms in a disused shed in Wexford,
Westport in the light of Asia Minor,
the black lace fan your mother gave you,
one February morning, the face in the mirror.

But as you go, watch out for Wordsworth's daffodils,
Yeats' nine bean rows, and nine-and-fifty swans,
the view into nothingness Robert Frost reveals
when he has his homebound heart-sore narrator stop
just three lines in 'to watch the woods fill up with snow'.

And if you can't find snow, there's always static,
background radiation, the wormhole swirl
when the bath water drains, the random thoughts
you notice passing through your head
when your mind is elsewhere.
Live with uncertainty. Time began and will end.
Invest in a hard-backed notebook and a good pen.

Walk in the footsteps of others as far as they go,
till page-blindness, word-deafness hits you, till words fall slow
and far apart, then not at all, leaving you there
at the end of your tether of footprints
in the bright, cold air.

At the edge of sense and meaning,
with your ear to the ground, make sound
judgements. See how the world hesitates
close to the truth, how youth and passion speak
in monosyllables, while the sly politician
comes wrapped in his Latinate cloak.

Make poems, a voice whispers. Own the language.
Fill the page or screen with what's within reach.
Who fails in the morning may later still succeed
when the cattle and children are sleeping,
when the last of the light goes limping over the fields
and the sky dons its mourning headdress
to bathe in the loss.

O daughters of Eve, says the voice, O sons of Uisneach,
O people of the iPad and the mobile phone,
of the banking collapse and rising unemployment,
don't leave it to those who claim to know where they're going,
when they're expected, what's on the menu for tea.

This time, no excuses. The story begins
where you are; the poem sets off through the woods
with a lunch packed by Emily Dickinson, word by careful word,
beauty, strangeness and mystery in every direction.

What's that noise? A bird in the canopy,
a telephone ringing? Concentrate now.
Blink and you miss it. Risk it. Don't be afraid.
The worst that can make it into ink
has all your life been singing in your head.

COLM BREATHNACH

An Ní Sin

Amhail éan
a phléascfaí as a chéile
san eitilt do
ag an ngrán,

falla caisleáin
go mbainfí faoi
san oíche

nó grianghraf
a stróicfí ina bhlúirí
ag buirgléir
gan chúis
na cuimhní go léir agam díot
mar gheall ar nár labhramar
in aon chor i dtaobh an ní
nár labhramar faoi.

Amhail éan
a phléascfaí as a chéile
san eitilt do i lár an lae ghil.

That Matter

Like a bird
blasted apart
in flight
by the shot,

a castle wall
undermined
in the night

or a photograph
ripped to pieces
by a burglar
needlessly,
all the memories I have of you
because we didn't ever
speak about the matter
we never spoke of.

Like a bird
blasted apart
in flight in the middle of a bright day.

Dán Cam

A Chéirseach
bíonn gal ar d'anáil
nuair a labhraíonn tú liom

agus i dtaobh éigin
tá fonn mall
á sheimint as tiúin.

Séideann an ghaoth
ár mbréithre go léir
chun na mara
mar ghaineamh.

A Chograigh
nuair a fhéachann tú orm
bíonn dusta i do rosca,

i bhfogas dom
rinctear polca
gan fothram cos,

agus caitheann an aimsir
na haighthe fidil go léir
a chaithimid
ceann i ndiaidh a chéile
ar nós na dtonn
ag trá go mall.

Crooked Poem

My husky love
when you speak
your breath is smokey

and somewhere
a slow air
is played out of tune.

The wind blows our words
out to sea like sand.

Sweetheart
when you look at me
there's dust in your eyes

and nearby
a polka is danced
with no stamping

and time wears
all the masks
we wear
one
after
the
other
like the waves
ebbing
slow.

PADDY BUSHE

Black Dogs

for John P.

Hilarity, yes, but also the only-half-smiling
Faces and tears of the counsellors
As we followed the wheelbarrowed body
Of the addiction centre's house dog
To the hedgerowed corner of the field.
Cara. Friend. Its name resonated
As the still shining black body
Was tipped easily into the grave.

I remember how I longed for a friend,
An *anamchara*, that first evening
As we filed back to therapy, each one
Of us digging deep in the clay
Of our own thoughts, each one
Aching to bury our own black dog.

Talbot Grove, 25 April 2007

January

That is no season for the margins, the thin
Forlorn cries of seabirds along an empty shore,
The exhausted light turning a haggard face
To the overwhelming clouds, and the sodden clay
Of the retreating cliff falling in dribs and drabs.

I will go inland awhile, accept the shelter of woods,
The texture of bark and knotted twigs, will ease
Myself into the dark of leaf-mould, nut-mast,
And become familiar with warm, hidden stirrings
Among the blind, white protuberances of bulbs.

Waiting

When fog freezes heart's landscape
And stops the veins and wells, and drains
The colour from everything that grows,
Oh then heart must kernel its sweet self
In hiding from the hooded crow, and wait
For hints of sap. Then thaw. Then flow.

PHILIP CASEY

Stadium

A new stadium was built
and it was popular
and the local crime graph
plummeted.

Then, like a roadside bomb,
a fist the size of six men
burst through the mid-field turf
throwing up players like rag puppets.

Where had the anger come from?
How long had it been there?
How long would it endure?

Cruelty

When you were a child,
a veil closed around your life.

Later, yes, you could see through it, but
when you reached out to love,
all you could see were lips move
in silence.

All your life you were like a cat
in a bag, but no one threw you
over the parapet. They thought

you were laughing, just like them.
It was only years later that you understood
that you, too, were cruel.

It wasn't the cruelty of inflicting pain;
that, in at least one instance,
might have been humane.

It was the cruelty of not being present
to one who wanted you, wanted all of you.
And there was nothing you could do.

HARRY CLIFTON

Going Feral

Only here, at the head of a pack of hounds
In a tenement room, on a patch of waste ground

Everything, man or animal, might share,
Did the humans, telling her she was not all there,

Abandon her forever or a while
To wander the forest of cities, like a child

Suckled on wolf's milk, smelling of dog,
Unable to defend herself, or beg

In a common language. Knowing the Word
But no grammar. Panting in surds

At the packs of the concerned – the half-sisters,
Half-brothers, cloned from the masters,

Finding her where they left her, curled
In the forgotten corner of a lost, unfallen world.

MICHAEL COADY

News from the Sky

Switch off the clamour and take
the path by the river. There's Teresa
before you, face turned up
to the sky from her wheelchair.

– They're back this last week. Isn't it
a wonder to God how they can
make it all that way every year?

Follow her eyes, take in aerobatics
this given evening between
the river and Poorhouse Field.

– And even to the same nests if they're
still there. The old people used to say
evict a swallow and your cow goes dry.

Helpless, downy they enter the world
says the guide. We're helpless too –

our coming and leaving
utterly bare.

Hirondelle, fáinleog, la golondrina,
outflanker
of winter

and over flyer
of all human
history,

well
come
here.

EVELYN CONLON

The Long Drop

Thomas McGurk knew that people got more confident with age, that they were able to tackle the small matters in life as if they were what they were. Or he thought he knew. But herein lay a problem, he wasn't sure anymore if what he knew or thought he knew was right. Indeed he knew nothing for certain these days, and appeared to have mislaid his nerve. Take his last visit to the dentist. He had punched in his time in the waiting room building himself up, speaking positively to himself. But then a stray thought had donated itself. If Mr Rattigan said to him this time,

'Oh dear, there is no problem with your teeth, but your gums, your gums!! Your teeth will last you your lifetime, but your gums! Mind you, your lifetime, hmmm, still smoking I see, hmmm ...'
he would say,

'Look here, you're my dentist, that's all, and I'm paying you to look after my teeth, to service my mouth so to speak, so stop your lecturing and get on with the job.'

But he only *wanted* to say that, he wouldn't, he hadn't got the nerve. And he used not mind what the dentist said, but now he had actually become afraid of that lecture, unable to answer it. He should say,

'See here you Mr Rattigan, I do not think it's any of your business what I do with my mouth or any other part of me. Stick on your gloves and your protective mask and floss away to your heart's content. And by the way, could you cease making provocative statements while my mouth is being held open by the mini walking stick that you've just thrown over my teeth.'

Dead, that's the only way he'd ever say it. For the last six months he couldn't say boo to a goose.

This might be a problem for any person, but for Mr McGurk

it was a disaster because his job was in PR. 'That's right,' he thought, 'I'm supposed to be a PR man. A man who knows everything, a constantly busy, important man.' The queue dwindled slowly. He was glad of this and yet he wanted to be out of here. Decisive! He was also having nightmares. In the last one he had been a participant in a simple quiz show on television. He had answered only one out of thirty five questions. Sweat had poured down the screen. The whole country had been watching him, including his first girlfriend and unrecognisable other girlfriends whom he never knew he had.

Waking up had not brought him consolation, had instead worried him further. A PR man. A man who knows everything, a man who can be handed any fact, who can then take that fact away on a private walk and do with it whatever he wants, a man who is too busy to notice the unimportant goings on of the ordinary unimportant people who walk up and down his road. So what had this exceptionally important man achieved so far that day?

Breakfast had been eaten quickly, the less said the better being his motto at that hour in the morning. On one side of him was his good-looking son who picked his way through cereal, and everything else, as if he owned the world and had bought the table. Yes, the less said the better. On the other side of him his ageing, his old, father who was visiting for a week. Thomas McGurk was being storm destroyed, youth and senility were filling his arteries this morning, leaving no time for his own age. He had then gone to Foreign Exchange at the bank. The customer in front of him was talking twenty to the dozen, telling all her business. Maybe she was a widow and had no one to talk to at home? The bank teller appeared to be listening. The customer told him loudly, cheerfully, at the top of her voice range like a chorister, that she wanted separate pesetas for the two children, for their own pocket money, you know what I mean, plenty of notes if possible, preferably not the ten thousand ones, this by way of explaining that she did know roughly the denominations in question. Or that she had children, or that she was going, could afford to go, on a holiday. What was he doing listening to this claptrap, what was he doing coming into the bank in the first place, when he had more important things to be doing?

'That was a terrible accident,' she said. 'Of eleven of them only seven were found, they were killed as well as drowned.'

He was in the bank getting sterling for his trip to London. He could use his card and get it out of a machine at the other end, but banks could be comforting; going to Foreign Exchange marked the importance of country leaving, set differences between one journey and another; it would be a terrible thing if they ever brought in the *ecu*. Or he could easily have asked his wife to get him the money, for some reason she had the height of respect for him, the last person to suffer from that, he hiccuped to himself.

He went to the counter, did his business, chatted amicably enough to the clerk, got his changed money. Such a transaction! This paper is worth that. Now can you give me someone else's paper worth the same. And different people accrued different amounts of paper for living the same lives. There was a lot to Marx.

He should be looking at the ads on the wall, he was a PR man, he should be interested. But he could only look at the woman sitting at the back desk in the office, not that he thought her good-looking, but because she seemed so organised, so engrossed, she must be content. There was a flawless rhythm about the way she lifted the telephone, tapped her computer, put down the phone, reached for papers, for statements, and it was herself who had worked out that rhythm. Yes, he should be interested in the ads, maybe he could make an ad out of her. He didn't make ads as such, but keeping the new successful ones just under his skin at his temple was part of his job in PR. The successful ad would tell you how to pitch your next product. A good PR man could sell anyone anything, could make anyone believe. He used to be able to do so himself. And now. Now he had to hesitate before having a conversation with his wife. This would have to stop. After seeing the dentist, he would go to the office, find out what his duties were to be in London, some new contract. He would cheer up, cheer himself up, take his wife out to dinner, pack his clothes for tomorrow, sleep well, have no dreams.

That must have been three months ago, no, longer than that, because it was while in London that it had really started, or maybe that's when he had noticed just how smack bang up against wall he was. The day had been ridiculously hot for May, from his window the street looked like a cramped smoky pub. There must have been a shortage of air because people had paused by railings, when they found them, and gasped, as if they were in hospital corridors. He left his hotel to go see de Kooning at the Tate, almost rhymed with Beckett at the Gate, a poem he'd just read. He'd started to do this recently, first it was to impress clients, or coPRers. de Kooning at the Tate would sound good. But there was a danger that some of it could seep in, that he would find himself standing in front of a picture longer than was necessary, that he would begin dropping into bookshops casually, that he would begin to believe poems.

He'd read about the de Kooning in *The Independent,* the English one, *on Sunday.* At home in bed. He came to the Arts pages last, usually at twelve thirty or so, that's Monday really, but it still feels like a Sunday night. Tight, choked, a hot London street. A few minutes after the Arts pages comes the 'How We Met', he hated it, just as much as he used to hate 'Family Ties' in the *Sunday Tribune,* where one family member waxed on about another, shone things up, glossed over their real selves. He knew the tricks. He knew a man who had done it once, he had tried to be analytical, he said, but they had managed to change the tone by letting a word or two slip, or so the man said, but Thomas didn't believe him. He happened to know that the man hadn't spoken to his brother for years, that there was a rotting thing between them, a thing that would have been smellable from the next townland if they'd lived in wide open spaces where smells could be separated. Thomas didn't know much about de Kooning, nothing in fact, he didn't mind admitting to himself, but he liked the name and got fixated for the few moments that it took him to read the article. He checked the dates. He would go see it on his next visit to London, it would fit in. He considered these fixations to be every bit as reasonable as love.

So there he was now on the tube, reading the bad thriller he'd bought at the Airport. Even his wife had done more dangerous things in her life than the woman who had got herself murdered in the book. He lifted his eyes too often to check the next station, the names not staying with him long enough, making him look like a stranger. He was a stranger. Last month he'd gone to the hospital with his father, supposedly to find out for the rest of the family what these tests would say, what exactly the matter was, but he had skulked in the waiting area for as long as possible, not wanting to be told about body parts, nor hear his father talk about this and that and sigh that ten years ago there hadn't been too much wrong with him. Before setting off for the appointment he'd had a moment of caring and had offered to bring breakfast to bed for the old man, but of course his father had insisted on getting up to have it with him, stealing his privacy, telling him to lift that good coat, making him a child in front of his own child, who didn't notice either of them. There was a new nightmare that came often, the coat hangers rattling on the back of their bedroom door, signalling his father walking in on top of them. In the hospital his father had looked at the man across the room,

'Put you in mind of Mary's Liam.'

'I don't know,' Thomas had snapped, and then tried to take the sting away by attempting to laugh: 'And couldn't care less.'

How brave of him to be bullying an old man. He was nearly overcome by the grief of not caring. He knew that the old man's neighbour took two hot water bottles to bed but kept the windows and doors open for fresh air. Very important that. How he knew was obvious, he had been told. Many times. For what reason he didn't know. Ridiculous womanish things that the old man would have told his wife if she had still been alive, most likely it was her who had said them in the first place and he was repeating them now to his personal vacuum. He'd been told lots of other things too, of no importance any of them, clogging up thinking space and the telling of them clogging up time. He needed a personal drainage system from his brain, he knew so much useless information. When your head got full of useless information did you keel over? Did old really mean a head more full of memory than expectation?

His father had made a county council cottage into a thing almost resembling a bungalow, so surely Thomas could be a PR man. He would PR his way out of every corner. Remember that brave boy who had jumped into the dying bus driver's seat and slammed on the brakes in time to stop a catastrophe? It was on the TV. Apparently he couldn't be brave again and it was expected of him. Word is, he couldn't repeat himself, well neither could Thomas. Thomas had lost his PR skills.

In the ward, where they settled his father into a bed, more tests to be done, the old man prattled away the nervous waiting and Thomas knew not of what he spoke. He was a stranger indeed.

He got off at the right station and went to the art gallery where he saw a woman who walked around beautifully, the trousers clinging to her, like silk does to a woman. Watching her was almost unbearable. In truth he was glad to get out of the de Kooning. The painter neither upset nor pleased him. He went to a cafe where he watched his accent – you could never tell the temperature of Anglo-Irish relations. It was best to avoid confrontation. He got sad for himself. Could loneliness get worse than this? He was growing for his grave, waiting around to have his name fitted on a headstone. Of course he was a PR man. But what did that mean? When he was young, a woman had disappeared from his parish, a woman not quite right, leaving behind a brother who was even less right. A telegram arrived, 'Miss Mary Bell Alive And Well In

Belgium.' Her brother repeated it like a mantra down through the years. A man his own age, who became a European, saw the same Mary Bell, destitute in Brussels, at the age of sixty. He decided to tell no one, except Thomas. It would be better for neighbours to think of her as alive and well. Thomas wished that he hadn't been told.

After the café, Thomas went to his meeting. The client wanted to advertise in Ireland, the economy was doing well there, the papers said so. He wanted a space theme, what did Thomas think? What did Thomas think about space? Here's what he thought. He couldn't cope with his own sitting room. The client had been in Ireland ten years ago. He asked questions appropriate to that experience and for a few moments Thomas was fine. The tricks of happiness include explaining to strangers the politics of one's country to one's own satisfaction, leaving out the aggravating truths. In Berlin and Jerusalem this is allowed, places where it is clear that there is no such thing as the truth, that all truth depends on perspective. In the client's office, for five minutes, Thomas talked like a citizen of one of those cities, or Belfast. In hotels at night, in strange countries, you can draw maps to show the bar-staff where you were born in relation to Dublin and the Border. They won't know that you've got the shape of the country all wrong.

The client looked like his brother-in-law, the one who had ME. All those years in bed had given his brother-in-law a young look. Had this man had ME, or was he in fact just young? What did this client know about Ireland? Did he know that they were now growing pot plants in the country, for God's sake? Thomas had noticed them on his last journey to the Midlands, where he'd stayed in a damp hotel. The local radio station had blared over the system at breakfast, he had been forced to listen to the funeral arrangements for the coming two days. Soon he wouldn't have to worry about his teeth being gone, they would just be gone. When he was young he was always out making things happen. There had been a vastness of time in front of him, he could have been anything, he could have become gay, could have become a light person.

'We will go out and make things happen,' the client said.

'Indeed we will,' said Thomas, buttoning up his coat, snapping closed his briefcase, backing out the door, afraid to walk face first. Going through the swing doors, he thought: 'I don't want to actually be a bird, I just want to fly.'

On the street a church bell rang continuously as if six funerals were arriving. A singing busker looted her life for the emotions of her song. If she were on a real stage could she have ambition? Thomas used to have that, unfailingly dependant desire to master the next goal, to get the next most important job, to meet important people. And he had met them. But the trouble is that when you know hordes of people you know more people who get sick, and more people who die. He had been good at his job, very good, so good he was hated. Not for him the useless pity of the encyclopedia seller who tells the destitute pensioner that, on second thoughts, she cannot afford his books. If there was a man in the room who might be useful some time he got buried in him in two seconds flat. And made sure that no one else got near him. Now getting a taxi was an achievement. But if he got one maybe he could stay in it. Not yet.

Thomas saw a church and sidled in. He had left all that palaver behind him ages ago. The smell was still the same. The silence was still the same. That's what he needed. Silence. Total silence. He had talked too much in his lifetime, laid silence to waste in his job. All those sentences. The air was still the same. He sat in the back row and fell asleep. If he expired here, they would whisper to each other at home, 'Did you hear that he died in the chapel. That's a good one, isn't it.'

SUSAN CONNOLLY

The Ghost House

Years ago
I broke all the mirrors
in this house,
and I hurled myself
through a closed window
to breathe cold air.

Unhurt,
with a piece of mirror
no bigger than a coin,
with the sharpest shred of glass
I could find –
I began my journey.

In this world I have cut
quite a long path since then –
visible only to myself.
At every crossroads
I have drawn blood.

With the small oval mirror
I catch the sun's full
strength, and I can see
my green eyes – but never
my whole self at once.

Pass by my window
in winter;
you are sure to see
the fire dying –
and the empty chair.

ENDA COYLE-GREENE

Birdsong

After the party,
lights out,
curtains closed,
the town is still
asleep as he awakens
pavement dust.

The backdrop
to the Mournes
paled to grey,
the sea a murmur
known to no one else,
he finds himself

surprised –
not by shadows, absences
there, all around him
at this hour;
those footsteps
are his own.

Night remains,
but it's stained
by the day that is
ravelling slowly
from loneliness,
birdsong.

TONY CURTIS

Two Poems in Memory of Elizabeth Bishop

1. OF THEE I SING

The border guard came down through the carriage,
all the way from America. Elizabeth, six and already lost,
studied the silver watch chain on his big belly rise
and fall as he bent to check each traveller's papers.

When he stood above her and her grandfather,
she noticed two buttons on his shirt were missing,
and a tuft of fine grey hair was sprouting,
as if a mattress had burst its gut. As the guard

bent to scrutinize their papers, the morning sun cut
slant across her grandmother's tired face.
Elizabeth would never lose that lit moment:
the mattress enquiring whose child she was

and her grandmother's whispers: *My dead son's child,*
mother lost in a wilderness of grief, Great Village, Nova Scotia,
no great place to raise a child, and besides – louder now –
she was born in Massachusetts, she's an American girl.

We're teaching her American ways, American tunes,
Shenandoah, My Country, 'Tis of Thee.
The guard looked at the lost and motherless child,
then asked Elizabeth if she was happy to be back in America?

'No,' she said, 'it's the land where my father died.'

2. LEAVING ST. ELIZABETH'S

This is the house in Nova Scotia.

This is the child
who sleeps in the house in Nova Scotia.

This is the year
of the tragic mother
who screams in the house in Nova Scotia.

This is the train
leaving today.
Grandparents are taking the child
away from the house in Nova Scotia.

This is the guard
checking the papers
of the small child sitting so quiet.
The grandmother says she belongs
away and away from the house in Nova Scotia.

This is the border crossing
from Canada to America.
All show your papers,
all smile at the guard.
No one mention her mother;
she screams in the house in Nova Scotia.

These are the years of electro-shock therapy.
There are sparks in her ears,
there is a gag in her mouth.
She rarely screams now,
only in dreams.

She wakes to the morning
miles from the house in Nova Scotia

This is the madwoman in the yellow hat.
She danced in Massachusetts
all over the dancehall floor.
There are photographs of her smiling
in black and white.
Her husband was buried
while the band played
and she danced through the house in Nova Scotia.

This is the library.
The madwoman
in the yellow hat,
she never goes there.
She is too busy dancing
with sailors and girls.
Her brain got fried with the bacon.
They eat it for breakfast every morning
with eggs at the house in Nova Scotia.

This is the girl, Elizabeth.
She lies on the floor all day
dead drunk, in her window
is the world, it is outside
and will always remain that way.
She weeps for the flowers,
she waltzes with the bees
that buzz through her window.
She hears them humming to the madwoman
she's leaving to her screams at the house in Nova Scotia.

These are the years, the rooms and the door
that closed on the girl, the child Elizabeth
who lies on the floor.
This is the madwoman in the yellow hat,
she dances through the corridors
to the locked door
and shakes her fist
at the dirty window
at the small face,
at the poet, the girl
who is leaving the house in Nova Scotia.

This is the mother who never came home.
These are the years, the rooms and the doors
the girl sits loose at the bar
and asks for vodka or gin,
something to take the pain away.
She would join the men on the dance floor
but for the woman in the coffin,
and the madwoman by the door. Show the guard
the papers, ask what time the train gets in,
the madwoman's going all the way
she's screaming down the tracks
screaming from the old house in Nova Scotia.

PÁDRAIG J. DALY

Bill

A friend who took his own life

He did not hear the birds sing this morning,
Nor the waters whisper along the dykes.

He did not notice how splendidly the rising sun
Was recreating the sheepcovered hill.

He did not think of the small boy,
The wife, the girls he left sleeping.

In a world of light
He trekked a deep tormented darkness.

In the middle of love
No love could reach him.

On a broad mountain
He walked a dark tunnel,

Untouched by spring, untouched by hope,
From which there was no exiting.

Ramparts

First, the ramparts;
Then, below the ramparts,
The ever-in-and-out of the sea.

A gull cries.
Somebody in the distance plucks strings.
Behind us, the town falls back towards the hills.

Men come from doorways
With effigies of the tortured Saviour.
People kneel in the streets, sing rawthroated songs.

Out on the inhospitable rocks, a gannet drifts onto sky.

PHILIP DAVISON

Bang
a short play

WAVERING YELLOW LIGHT, A BARE STAGE, The exaggerated
sound of a deep-fat fryer.

*JAS, a big man in his fifties, moves erratically about the stage. He has
a bag of chips in his hand, which he seems to have forgotten.
MARIANNE, a slight woman in her early twenties, enters carrying a
tape recorder. Her arrival further agitates Jas, but she is not surprised
by this and attempts to corral him. He stumbles. She manages to break
his fall. The chips are saved. Jas suddenly becomes preoccupied with
the space above his head.*

JAS: Buzzzzz.

MARIANNE: What? Again?

JAS: Yes. Again.

MARIANNE: Where.

JAS: Around my head. Where else?

MARIANNE: It'll pass.

JAS: Buzz. Up out of the grass into the blue. Then
                – bang.

MARIANNE: Bang. Yes. You've told me.

JAS: With the newspaper. Do you want a piggy-
                back? Is that it?

MARIANNE: No, Dad.

JAS: You'd like a piggy-back, Marianne. You would.

He makes ready to get down on all fours.

MARIANNE *(forcefully)*: I'm too old, Jas.

Jas straightens; the sound of frying fades.

JAS: Your mother – she'll be on her high horse.

Marianne activates the tape recorder. We hear a bang – a rolled newspaper striking something hard. A cry of frustration from Jas on the tape.

Jas begins to trudge in circles. Marianne keeps pace.

MARIANNE: I have you.

JAS: This is torture.

MARIANNE: But I want more.

JAS: Do you?

MARIANNE: You need to hear yourself. Length and breadth.

JAS: Look up. Look up.

MARIANNE: Mind where you're going.

JAS: Navigation, Marianne. Up there. Down here. I'll show you someday. Can't show you now because – well, you know – I'm –

MARIANNE: I know what you are. Mind my mother's chips.

He holds out the bag; looks to the sky. The YELLOW LIGHT TURNS TO AZURE.

JAS: Mind. Yes. Salty stars. Hope it doesn't rain.

MARIANNE: It's the middle of the day, you eejit.

JAS:	It used to be your mother came looking for me. Now, she stays at home and makes it rain. You've a lot to learn, Marianne. Remember your old Dad said that.
MARIANNE:	I will. I'll remember. Paint me a picture.
JAS:	Home in time for the boxing?
MARIANNE:	Now he's trying to be funny.
JAS:	Bang.

Marianne activates tape –

JAS ON TAPE:	I'm going down the road. Do you want chips?
JAS:	I have the chips. There's the chips. I'm bringing home the chips. You hunt me down with your tape recorder, but I have the chips.
MARIANNE:	I have to take time off work for this.
JAS:	Buzzzzzz.
MARIANNE:	Here you are – wandering around. People think nobody cares about you.
JAS:	I've been drinking again.
MARIANNE:	That's why I have the recorder.
JAS:	You want to embarrass me.
MARIANNE:	I'm sorry it has come to this. Whatever's gnawing away at you, drinking isn't the solution.
JAS:	You could play me music instead of recording.
MARIANNE:	Too late.

He stops suddenly, bends down, jesting he's ready again to make a piggy-back. Marianne throws a mock punch. He gently rolls to the ground.

MARIANNE & JAS: Bang.

JAS:	Marianne, don't be promising people you've something juicy on your tape machine. Something about us and the way we live and what's important. Don't be.

Marianne activates the tape –

JAS ON TAPE:	Don't be, don't be, don't be.
JAS:	Don't be – doing that.
MARIANNE:	All right. Just sit there. Get swatted.
JAS:	Don't haunt me.

Marianne activates the tape –

JAS ON TAPE: Haunt me.

MARIANNE:	We've heard it all before – haven't we, Dad?
JAS:	Bang.

Marianne activates the tape –

JAS ON TAPE:	Bang.
MARIANNE:	Bang.
JAS:	I've had it, haven't I? I'm flattened. I'm squashed.
MARIANNE:	No, you're not. Get up on your feet. We miss you.

She helps him to his feet. They begin circling in the opposite direction.

JAS:	Those chips are cold.
MARIANNE:	Never mind.
JAS:	It's my fault – the chips.
MARIANNE:	*That's* not important. I'm going to tell you what's important.

JAS:	No. Don't. It'll only make me feel bad.
MARIANNE:	And you don't feel bad?
JAS:	It'll make me feel worse. You can always feel worse. Play your tape and I'll feel worse.
MARIANNE:	At least we're on our way.
JAS:	The chips are fecked.
MARIANNE:	Stop.
JAS:	I get the chips. I'm on my way home, then, something happens, and I have to have a few drinks. Just give me a minute.
MARIANNE:	A minute? What for?
JAS:	A minute to atone.
MARIANNE:	Heard that before.
JAS:	DON'T turn that thing on. I'm doing my best. This atoning is not like the last atoning. I'm atoning afresh. All right? Your mother's chips are cold and it's my fault.

Marianne activates the tape –

JAS ON TAPE:	My fault – your mother's chips are cold.
JAS:	Stop.
MARIANNE:	Don't you know we love you, Dad?
JAS:	Stop with the torture. Please. My mind isn't right.
MARIANNE:	I want to help. We can go to somebody.
JAS:	Play them the tapes?
MARIANNE:	The tapes are so you know what you sound like when you drink.

JAS:	You keep telling me that. And I keep at it. It's the mind. This mind.
MARIANNE:	Look, I've got to get back to work. I'm late as it is. What do you think I say to my boss? 'Boss, sorry I'm late. I had to torture my Dad.'

Jas stops suddenly; gets down on all fours –

JAS:	M'on, love. Hop on.

Marianne activates the tape –

JAS ON TAPE:	Do you want a piggy-back? Have a piggy-back. Get your Mam. I'll carry the both of you. Get on. Get on. Is there nobody working with me?
JAS:	Stop.
MARIANNE:	He's on the ground again. I've hours of this stuff.
JAS:	Don't talk to strangers.
MARIANNE:	M'on.
JAS:	Get on for a piggy-back. I'll take you all the way home. I had chips myself. They've made me big and strong again.

Marianne pushes him over with her foot. He laughs.

	Now you're with me.
MARIANNE:	Love you, Dad. Up you get.
JAS:	Do I hear buzzing?
MARIANNE:	You will if you don't get up. Have you no pride left?
JAS:	I do. I have. I promise.

She helps him to his feet. It seems they can't walk. They stand shoulder to shoulder.

MARIANNE:	There now.
JAS:	There now. You see. Proud again. Bang away.
MARIANNE:	Bang? Listen – I *have* to get back to work.
JAS:	And I'm delaying you. I'm sorry.
MARIANNE:	Mam and me – we're only trying to help.
JAS:	I know.
MARIANNE:	But, we're tied.
JAS:	I know you are. I am too.
MARIANNE:	I bring this recorder into work every day.
JAS:	I'm a disgrace.
MARIANNE:	I hear myself on the tape sometimes and I weep.
JAS:	Ah don't.
MARIANNE:	Then, I do more recording.
JAS:	Stop.
MARIANNE:	And, I play you the tape.
JAS:	I can't bear it.
MARIANNE:	But you tell us you don't say these things.
JAS:	Is it getting worse?
MARIANNE:	Why won't you talk to somebody?
JAS:	I talk to you.
MARIANNE:	We've lost you.
JAS:	My precious darling daughter. Never.
MARIANNE:	I'm fighting for you. Mam's fighting for you.
JAS:	I'm coming out of it. With a better head.

MARIANNE:	I have that on tape.
JAS:	Give up the recording. Have a little faith.
MARIANNE:	I recorded you saying that with your drinking buddy the day before yesterday.
JAS:	No you didn't.
MARIANNE:	Want to hear?
JAS:	No.
MARIANNE:	No lunch for me again.
JAS:	You can do all sorts of torture with tape. You can chop it up. Make people say what they didn't.
MARIANNE:	There's been no chopping.
JAS:	You can add terrible sounds.
MARIANNE:	It's unabridged. It's in the raw.
JAS:	Is that buzzing I hear? Is somebody going to get flattened?

Marianne activates the tape –

JAS ON TAPE:	Have a little faith. Have a little faith.
JAS:	It's getting worse.
MARIANNE:	How often do I tell you I'm with you, Dad? I'm on your side. We'll make it better together – you, me and the tape.
JAS:	Bang.
MARIANNE:	It doesn't have to be bang.
JAS:	You haven't had your lunch, love. Have the chips.
MARIANNE:	No chips for me. Will we see you later?

JAS: You will.

MARIANNE: You'll be all right?

JAS: I will.

Jas trudges away, on his own circle. Marianne activates the tape –

JAS ON TAPE: I will. I'll be all right. Promise.

MARIANNE: No bang.

JAS *(calling back)*:   No bang.

Marianne activates the tape –

JAS ON TAPE: Buzzzzzzz.

Jas breaks into a trot, then, a shambling run.

MARIANNE *(calling)*: Mind yourself.

Jas suddenly EXITS

Marianne activates the tape –

MARIANNE ON TAPE: Bang. He's gone.

Marianne EXITS. LIGHTS WAVER, THEN FADE.

– END –

GERALD DAWE

One Evening

No end to the strimming,
the APÉ buzzes its way through
winding streets and under balconies
where bright bed-sheets rustle
like flags. In the clammy room,
not a shred of light, not a bird or voice,
only your steady breathing away
deep down in your own dream world.

The still of evening – a grey evening,
it has to be said – slates of the house
beyond have loosened, a slate-grey
pigeon luffs by and from the kitchen,
the washing machine's final cycle
spins faster and faster like so many lives.

JOHN F. DEANE

Dolores

We mocked her, for her withered hand,
her side-legging walk, her hare-lip, her stammering;

we were, all of us, guilty, and knew it; save when
after Mass, she opened shop and we came seeking

thruppence-worth, or sixpence, or a penny –
fruit pastilles and hard gums, lucky bags and liquorice pipes –

then was she mistress, for the nonce,
of weights and measures, of paper bags and paper pokes,

playing her jingle-jangle till-music; woman
with a preference for dusklight, who would have danced

on this one earth, under bright chandeliers
but held desire fast in old account-books, their mouse-gnawed covers;

there is no geography to clarify such a life
from the wail out of the cramped womb to the silence; and what

do the scriptures say of life's banquet?
each guest and place at table, each delicacy, each sharp note stricken.

Ethel

Goldfinch on the thistle-heads, visitors skittering
on the hazels – redpoll, siskin, shrike – under the whitesilk
innocence of the blossoms, hawthorn limbs
are contorted in their growth. She walked the gardens, scarcely

present, her mind divided kingdoms; she was an irritable
zither, without strings, humming her no-rhythm no-tune hum;
withdrawal, her dream and her condition, hurt
by wars on the Atlantic, torpedoes and sea-shock; her lover

locked his love away from her till she came to hold
to the impossibility of earthly existence, turning and unturning
air between thin fingers, disliked the body and would hide
the mind from it. She was a sonata taken apart and the notes

scattered. And will the spirit, then, be driven out
with others, in haunted herds, across barren eternal plains?

PATRICK DEELEY

Cinéma Vérité

The Rathmines Stella, completely shot of its twinkle, is inherited,
now that we've done with it, by the meek – our 'feathered
   street rats' –
who rise flurrying from their pink-toed prance, to the grid
of rectangular spaces high in the granite brickwork, their very
   own loft.
We imagine them as the brains of the edifice, hatching movie
   plots –
cinéma vérité, not fluffy romance – in that stony cerebrum.
And the doubtful delights of mould and fleapit itch come
   scurrying back
from years ago, the moral guardianship of the usherette
shining her torch among our furtive kisses and gropes. Pigeon
   love,
dare we say this doesn't exist? – for look, they increase and
   multiply,
coo and preen, while their shelter, our forsaken den of dreams,
stays in the dark, no sunshine or exotic locations imaginable on-
   screen,
only dirt-stains and flimsy hammocks of spider-web hanging
where we watched the outlaw dismount from his het-up horse,
   the nurse
who'd seen too much of suffering administer a lethal dose,
the two soldiers play Russian roulette; – well, this audience roosts
unconcerned. The rumour of the street, a filtered whoosh, a
   beeping
car-horn, a gabble of voices rising behind us, won't stop them
settling for the night. And the plotlines of our lives – seemingly
   shapeless,

certainly untellable – move as we move, past steel-shuttered shop
and railing-rounded park, our prospects inauspicious, more
a case of earning the next crust than gazing at stardust, less intrigue
on the Orient Express than finding change for the last bus, yet
    somehow
to do with love, even to the grand, impossibly heroic gesture
we promise ourselves we would rise to in face of impending
    catastrophe.

Song for a Centenarian

The world will forget us, Josie, though we hold –
as you do – to one place for a hundred years;
the world is busy forgetting us even now as you lose
your bearings, fall down brittle-boned
in your little kitchen among the limestone hills,
and can neither lift nor drag yourself out

to daylight again. The crookedly hanging clock,
stained with turf-smoke, grease-spattered
from the frying pan, makes itself audible to you
as if for the first time. The concrete floor
coldly props your hip pain. The simple
sufficiency of bread, of milk in a jug, of a jar of jam,

stands unreachable. One hundred years
of stout health – call it forbearance or good fortune;
call it the knack of knowing how to pick
your step; or maybe it's the quiet rapture of always
feeling at home. Still there's no sizing
or summing life up; your purgatory of slow seconds

gathers into hours, into days; your panic settles
almost to repose at the sight of moonlight
illuminating the badly distempered chimney breast.
And this isn't the last, the end of anything,
but a continuing story where you survive, courtesy
of a square-shouldered bottle of whiskey

squatting on a low shelf, which you judiciously sip,
your head resting on the belly of the world,
your ear attuned for our footsteps. And hope – shyly
yet indefatigably you give it quavering voice –
is a bird breaking into song at dead of night,
prompting a tree to rise in the haggard of your mind.

GREG DELANTY

Wonder of Wonders

A girl cries. Her father beats her, convinces her she's dumb.
    She'll land back in that cave of herself again
and again for the rest of her life. So many are like mythical characters
    blindly returning to tackle whatever invisible monsters
brought them down so long ago in the Trauma Caves.
    Maybe the greatest wonder of wonders
of being alive – the lake like a glittering shield,
    the leaves turning tangerine, bronze, ruby
and so infinitely on – is, as yet, we have not undone our world.
    And should we each manage to wrestle
Trauma to the ground and tame him
    there is Thanatos – his natural father – waiting
at the end of it all, the Big-Wig behind the whole story.
    Time to give ourselves a pat on the back
for not having blown ourselves sky high.

THEO DORGAN

The Quiet Ones

Never had much to say for himself, Jimmy.
Teachers walked carefully around him, sensing the edge
on that considered silence, fearing that hooded look.
Evenings he'd walk the river with a book;
Zen poems, I remember, once on Lavitt's Quay
when our orbits crossed, myself a solitary by then,
my mind shot through with intimate doubts
and fears. I don't remember what we said,
but after that he'd nod if we met by chance
and I would feel steadied, a moment less unsure.
Somebody told me he walked into the river –
his silence, I do not doubt it, still intact.
The Zen of hopelessness. Cause and effect.

PAUL DURCAN

Thinking about Suicide

Although I may never commit suicide
I spend parts of each day thinking about suicide –
Thinking about how I lack the courage to do it.

I wake in the morning with 60% depression.
That's how it remains for the whole day
Except for the odd occasion in a year

In the doorway or on the street I meet by chance
For a few minutes a woman passing-by
Who has the time to stop and talk for three minutes

Or five minutes or even sometimes seven or eight minutes,
Who rocks back on her heels in her pink, hooped skirt
With laughter, no matter what the topic.

Depression and Despair are two different states
Of mind, not having a lot in common.
Although I have 60% depression, I do not despair.

I do not see eye to eye with Samuel Beckett
Who disapproved of suicide and who promulgated
The doctrine of 'going on' for the sake of 'going on'.

Estranged from my family, if I do not soon
Take my own life, others will take it from me –
Hooded males with knives in their track suits

Or medics in their scrubs prancing corridors
Or cowpat-faced ward sisters smirking
Or ice-cold proprietors of old people's homes.

How is it that you do not see it, Samuel,
That I do not want to go on for the sake of going on –
Seeing the same old, tired-out impressionist paintings again
    and again?

Men are such po-faced bores.
Each one of them an editor-in-chief.
I want to stand still by the water's edge.

I want to hold a woman's hand for the last time.
I want to fill my pockets with Palaeozoic stones.
I want to open my eyes.

CHRISTINE DWYER HICKEY

The Aviary

OURS WAS A LARGE BEDROOM. Formerly two rooms, knocked into one, it took up the entire top floor of a house we couldn't afford to live in. Four long windows overlooked the gardens: two to the back, two to the front and a blocked up fireplace stood at one end, over which hung a rust-mottled mirror. On winter nights the sash windows rattled us to sleep. In summer, with the long windows up, we could hear Mr Andrews' birds beeping like squeezed soft toys in their aviary. The three beds were doubles and, like the house, had been inherited from distant relatives of my father. Babies had been made and born in our beds, people had slept and died in them but I seemed to be the only one who lay awake at night and worried about such things. There were two wardrobes: a great big musty clump of mahogany shared by myself and Dora and another slimline, modern model that Tess had saved up for herself as soon as she started to work. My mother, who had a bad leg, couldn't manage the stairs without considerable pain, and so the bedroom became our own private world. On the rare occasion when my father did stick his nose round the door, he always made a remark about how you could park a bus in it. For all that, it never seemed big enough for Giovanna.

Before she arrived we knew only this about her – she was our first cousin, in her mid-twenties and had been born and raised on the continent. Her father was my mother's elder brother. She was called after my mother although Giovanna seemed miles away from Joan and felt more like a jelly sweet than a name, in my mouth.

Our room gleamed for her arrival. My mother's two sisters, Brenda and Margaret collected her from the train station and brought her to our house, where they puffed and panted up the three flights of stairs to help her unpack. They swooned over the beautiful clothes that came slithering out of her luggage, bleated with admiration at her accent, her perfume, her dancer's posture. They asked umpteen questions about her mother, her father and European living. And then they went back downstairs and left us to deal with each other.

Within days the mantle-shelf had filled up with her bits: combs, brushes, foreign cosmetics. Her clothes had bullied ours to the back of both wardrobes. There were coats and dresses lolling on the end of her bed and twirls of dirty underwear on the floor. Hats and scarves were heaped on the old kitchen table that Dad and Mr Andrews had hoisted up the three flights of stairs so Dora and I would have somewhere to do our homework and Tess could study the French she was taking at night school.

Giovanna was clotty. She could be rude in her comments and ungrateful in her manners. She thought nothing of locking herself in the bathroom for an age, leaving the rest of us to the stinky outdoor toilet with the wind hooshing under its door. But she shone her own peculiar light on the small routines of our lives. She dressed us in her clothes and jewellery; sprayed us with perfume and lacquer. She taught us bits of other languages; songs in German and French, Italian love-words and curses. She showed Dora how to do ballet pliés and how to dance sideways like an Egyptian. She drew our names in fancy letterings and gave Tess a beauty lesson in how to make her eyelashes black. She thrilled us to the bone with her Greta Garbo accent, telling stories of cocktails and cities and men.

My father sometimes talked to her about politics abroad or he might ask questions about the different people who called on her father. Mother took great care of her, giving her the best bits of meat which she seldom ate, and ironing her clothes that ten minutes later would be thrown in a ball on the floor. 'And how are you feeling now?' she would often ask, as if moments ago Giovanna had been poorly. Occasionally she called her into the parlour for 'a quick word in private'.

Giovanna was nearest in age to Tess but they didn't really hit it off. Nor did she have a whole lot of time for me which I presumed had something to do with my illness and the fact that I was too young for her. As it turned out she was at her best with Dora who, at ten years of age, was the youngest. She took her on afternoon outings and I was sometimes allowed to tag along – if Mother felt I was up to it. Even after two months convalescence I was still thought to be a bit 'dawny-looking' and in need of watching. I didn't feel dawny at all. I felt strong – if only they'd let me be strong. I felt I could run for miles across Dollymount Strand, swim all the way out to Howth. And I felt hungry. I wanted to eat all around me, pick up a whole wheel of cheese in my hands and gnaw my way through it. And I could never understand why, after a few running strides in the fresh air, my breath grew short and seemed to be trying to get back inside my lungs, or why, after a few mouthfuls of food, my stomach felt full and my tongue grew dead in my mouth.

She brought Dora and me to places we'd only ever seen from the outside: high-ceilinged banks where she changed foreign money; picture houses where she often left us alone for an hour or more. She left us again, outside a basement flat on Harcourt Street and when she came out, swore us to secrecy and then bought us cream buns for tea. On these outings strangers sometimes spoke to her; usually men. And once in Bewley's she pretended to one of them that we were foreign too and, as he spoke to us slow word by slow word, we nearly choked into our napkins trying to stop ourselves from laughing. Another time in Stephen's Green a man, older than my father, although much more handsome, asked her out to dinner.

Giovanna turned left and right in the mirror. Full profile, three quarters profile, hat on, hat off. She asked us again about the cast in her eye – was it more noticeable like this or like that? Did we think it spoiled her looks? Her chances of catching a husband then? It became a habit, this turning about in the mirror and asking about her eye.

And I thought it odd and even a bit mean of her, to go on and on about it, when both my sisters had a similar affliction: a family weakness which, until then, we had all more or less pretended not to notice.

'I just wish Giovanna didn't speak her mind quite so much,' I heard Mother say to my father one evening after Giovanna had told my Aunt Brenda that her new green coat made her look like a monument and then, when Tess's fiancé Pat was describing his job, interrupted to ask if it didn't make him weep with boredom.

'At the same time,' Mother continued, 'I just wish she'd give a little *more* of herself – you know this is her third refusal in a row to go to tea with Margaret.'

My father rattled his newspaper. 'More of herself! *More!* – Jesus, do you not think now we might have enough?'

⋍

It was the night before Tess went on her cycling holiday. I woke and saw Giovanna at the far end of the room looking into the fireplace mirror. Dora was fast asleep beside me and I was grateful to see Tess across the room, already awake and half-out of her bed.

'What are you doing?' Tess asked her

'Looking at them,' she said.

Tess switched on the lamp. A yellow gauze spread over the middle of the room and, behind it, I could see the back of Giovanna, long and thin in her nightie, her face a dim, watery mask in the mirror.

'Who?' Tess asked.

Giovanna said a few foreign words, stopped, then continued in English, 'I know they are in there. I almost see them. But when I look, they melt. And in a moment, I almost see them again.'

'For God's sake Giovanna!' Tess said, 'I'm supposed to be going on holiday tomorrow – in case you've forgotten. I need to sleep!'

I shut my eyes tight and snuggled back down into Dora's safe warmth. Tess got Giovanna back into bed and the night lamp went out and soon I could hear Tess's breathing deepen. But I knew Giovanna was lying there with her eyes wide open and I could hear the shivery sound of her whispers like someone praying in the dark.

I thought of the marble tiles on the wall of our bathroom and the things I saw in them anytime I sat on the toilet; groups of things. Yet I never saw the same group more than once. I tried to remember the last time: angels' heads growing out of a stalk and a man with a flat-cap and clouds and hair and a woman with no eyes and a pig's head like you'd see in the butcher's window.

⤴

Tess came back from her cycling holiday, took one look at the state of our bedroom and announced she was going to stay with the aunties. And we missed her so much, Dora and I, because even though she still popped in most days after work, she mostly stayed in the kitchen talking to Mother and refused to come up to our room. We were all so proud of Tess; she worked behind a counter in Brown Thomas and you couldn't get much swankier than that as my father liked to say. Sometimes when we went into town we would stand at the window and spy on her. It was something to show our friends from school. She might be serving a customer, or chatting to a colleague or polishing the glass on her counter: our big sister, with her slim hips and her high-heels, and her smart hairstyle and her long elegant hands with the twinkle of an engagement ring when she turned it under the light.

'The poshest shop in the whole city,' I heard Dora say to Giovanna on the bus into town. 'Oh wait till you see her!'

'I've already seen her,' Giovanna muttered without turning her head from the window.

'No, no, I mean in the shop. *In* it. I know you've already seen her and the shop too, but, but … See – she's back from her holiday now and you haven't, you didn't …' Dora broke off, unable to find the sense she'd been seeking. I could tell she was already worried that Tess behind the counter in Brown Thomas would prove to be a disappointment to Giovanna. I was on the seat behind and for the whole journey Giovanna, her face on the glass of the window, the curve of fur at her throat, her hat drawn down over one eye, didn't budge an inch. And for the first time I began to dislike my cousin. Dora kept talking to her, asking questions that remained unanswered, fidgeting excitedly on her seat, the bobble of her hat wobbling on the top of her head and Giovanna didn't say another word. I thought her false and spoilt then. And utterly selfish. I resented her for everything: her foreign voice and her film star clothes, and the way she always had to make heads turn whenever we walked into a café. The way she quizzed waiters as if they were her inferiors, then ordered food she hardly ate. The way she threw her money around but never bought so much as a bar of chocolate home for Mother. The way she bribed us to tell lies. But most of all for the way she had made Tess seem ordinary and had taken the adventure out of her cycling holiday, the romance out of her French lessons, the glamour off the man she would marry.

We came up near College Green and Dora stood up, placed one knee on the seat and, leaning into Giovanna, whispered. 'She won't be anywhere near as beautiful as you.'

And I felt like giving my little sister a slap. But I said, 'Sit down Dora – you'll fall.'

I became afraid of Giovanna. I found myself checking through the crack in the door before entering a room, to see if she was in it, and if she was I'd mumble an excuse and scuttle back out again. Then she stopped sleeping, and because there was something unsettling about the thought of her being awake, while I was asleep, I stopped sleeping too. The only rest I had was when she went out for the evening. Then I'd go up to bed early and immediately pass out. But as soon as I heard the doorknob turn, my eyes would pop open again. Sometimes she'd sit and frantically smoke a cigarette at the front window as if expecting someone to call. Or maybe she'd just stand staring into the mirror again. Mostly she'd just do what I was doing which was lie on my back, wide-awake, silent, gazing up at my own little patch of the ceiling.

Dora went back to school. It had been decided that a couple more weeks convalesence wouldn't do me any harm so I was kept home. And so, apart from Mother, who spent most of her time in the kitchen or pottering in the back garden, I found myself alone in the house with Giovanna. I tried to stay with Mother but she kept sending me off to keep Giovanna company or telling the pair of us to go out and get some fresh air and I had to keep pretending I didn't feel up to it and the more I pretended the worse I felt and the more dawny I looked and the longer I was kept out of school.

In the mornings Mother would send me up with a tray of milky coffee, bread and jam because that's all she would take for breakfast. If there was a letter from her father, I'd bring that up too. And I hated going up to our room on my own, the dread of her voice when I turned the last flight of stairs, singing to itself. Sometimes, I would see her head under the covers, pretending to be asleep, the sprout of her black hair on top, the whiff of ammonia which I later found out was the whiff of her medicine.

'What's she doing now?' Mother asked.

'She's singing, Mother.'

Well now, that's a good sign she must be a bit happier in herself so.'

But there was nothing happy about Giovanna's song, or the way she sang it, the same verse over and over.

In the kitchen we could hear her thundering over the long floor of our bedroom.

'Where's Her Highness?' Aunt Brenda asked, coming into the kitchen.

Mother lifted her hand and pointed twice to the ceiling.

'No sign of her going back then ....?'

'No.' Mother said.

'They've a cheek alright,' Margaret said following behind Brenda. 'I mean to say, have you not got enough to be doing?'

'He's asked me to keep her another while.'

'For God's sake, Joan – how much longer?' Brenda gasped. 'It's been over six weeks.'

'Well, he thinks it's good for her to be here and-.'

'Good for *her* maybe,' Brenda said.

'The way he sees it, she's been doing well, she has the girls for company and has even made a few friends. No disasters anyway, thank God.'

'Worse luck for you,' Margaret said rooting in her handbag and pulling out her fags

'What do you mean?'

'Well – are they going to leave her here for ever, just because she's been behaving herself?'

I went up to the hall and sat on the chair outside Mother's bedroom door and re-read the letter Tess had sent to me. It was written on Brown Thomas notepaper with a tiny drawing of the front of the shop on the top which I felt didn't do it much justice.

Tess said she was fed up with the aunties and their spinstery ways but better than putting up with Giovanna and her continental clottiness not to mention the way she treated Pat; either playing up to him or else being downright insulting.

I thought I heard something then at the top of the house and when I stood up and looked through the stairwell Giovanna was at the bannisters. For a minute I thought she was talking to me and, because I couldn't hear, began to climb the stairs. On the second flight, I saw then she was looking up, not down – her face turned to the skylight. She was talking to the air, wittering away to herself in a muddle of foreign words, like a wireless someone was trying to tune.

'Yes, but where does she go when she goes out in the evenings?' Aunt Margaret was saying when I came back down to the kitchen.

'She eats out.'

'What do you mean eats out? *Where?*'

'With her friends.'

'What friends?'

'All I know is she stays upstairs most of the day and –

'Doing what?' Brenda asked.

'Reading, drawing, sometimes dancing. Resting – he said she was to have plenty of rest. Then she comes down in the evening and goes out to meet her friends. And she seems fine and comes home at a reasonable hour. And that's good enough for me.'

'But the friends – who are the friends?'

'I'm her aunt not her jailer. And she's a grown woman, Margaret.'

'*Exactly*,' Aunt Margaret said.

⁓

In my dream one of the birds had escaped from Mr Andrews' aviary and the rest of the birds were screaming at it to come back inside. I could see them bouncing off the wire cage, their brittle claws catching on the mesh, their little heads turned sideways.

And then above all their angry racket, another, sharper sound – a peck on the window pane. And in the dream I said, oh no the escaped bird, what am I supposed to do now? how am I supposed to get it away from our window and back into the aviary? Another peck; harder this time and I thought, oh no it must be one of the bigger birds, and hoped not the cockatiel with its hooked determined beak that I'd seen tear the hand off Mr Andrews one time.

My eyes opened. My heart was drumming and my nightie was damp with sweat. I looked up at the window behind the bed but there was only a glaze of black sky above the lace half-curtain. The peck came again; a few seconds silence, then another one. I pulled myself up, reached across Dora and lifted the hem of the curtain; small stones on the window-sill. I pulled the curtain back and looked down into the garden. The sky was starting to redden and a slit of dawn-light was trying to get through. I saw plonked on the ground, near the outside toilet, her bag, coat, and one shoe. Then I saw Giovanna. She was rummaging for stones from Mother's ornamental border. The birds had quietened down, just the occasional squawk or squeal, and I guessed she had got through the side gap of Mr Andrews' gate, crossed his garden, then climbed over our high wall onto the roof of the toilet before dropping down. Giovanna stood up and gave a little stagger, steadied herself and staggered again – she was drunk. Giovanna drunk – if Mother could see her now.

I glanced down at Dora, still snoring away. A stone whacked off the window and I jumped. When I looked down, Giovanna was looking straight up at me; her clothes torn, her hair wild, a glitter in her eye.

Dora stirred in the bed and then woke. 'What is it?' she whispered

'Giovanna. She's drunk.'

'Drunk!?'

I let the curtain drop and moved to get out of the bed.

Then Dora grabbed my arm. 'Don't.' she said.

'But Dora?'

'Let her go round the front and ring the doorbell.'

'She'll waken Mother.'

'Let her.'

'Why?'

'I don't like her anymore.'

I slid back down into the bed and for a while Dora and I lay side by side holding hands. After a while the pecking stopped, or at least we fell asleep.

In the morning her bed was empty. I stared down into it, wondering what to do. The bed was unmade – as it usually was – and the letter that had arrived yesterday from her father was lying where she'd left it on the pillow. *Cara Mia*, it began and finished with *Bacci di Babbo*. I picked up the letter and studied my uncle's Irish handwriting, the same spindled slant as my mother and Tess, and then I read all the foreign words that he'd written, as if I could find a meaning or a hint in them, to where Giovanna might be.

It was Sunday morning; the house still quiet, I left Dora sleeping and tipped down the stairs, peeping into each room on the way and not a sign of Giovanna.

Mother's small garden was warming to the day; the grass spangled with dew, the flowers neat in their little beds, according to shape and colour. Giovanna's coat, shoe and bag were still on the ground. For a moment I hoped. But it was a small garden with no place to hide other than inside the toilet. I could see through the wide-opened door, nothing but the lime-crusted toilet and the long rusty chain. I stooped and with my hand brushed the scatter of pebbles off the garden path.

When I came inside Dora was shouting, 'Giovanna isn't here! Oh God, Giovanna! Giovanna! Where's Giovanna?'

⁻ᔡ

Once the policeman appeared, we spilled out the beans – the man in Stephen's Green, the afternoon we waited outside the flat on Harcourt Street; the times she left us alone in the picture house. Dora could only remember those details that directly concerned Giovanna – a joke she'd made or the fur coat she'd been pretending to buy. I remembered everything else; the colour of the suit on the man in Stephen's Green; the number of the door on Harcourt Street. I knew how much money and time she had spent and where she had spent it. I told about her staying in bed all day, about her whispering to herself in the middle of the night and about shouting at the woman in the chemist who wouldn't give her what she wanted. I told everything and anything I could recall except for the one thing that I would never forget nor mention again, not even to Dora. The sound of the stones pecking off the window and the birds from the aviary screaming in anger, and the sight of Giovanna gently swaying in our back garden, one arm reaching up to me, the flat of her palm stretched out.

⤳

A day later Giovanna was found although she never came back to our house. My father took the day off work and there were the voices of strangers in our parlour: policemen, a detective, a doctor in a pin-striped suit.

That evening her luggage was pulled down from the attic and the aunties puffed and panted back up all the stairs to our bedroom. Mother washed and ironed her dirty laundry, then insisted on carrying the stack up the stairs by herself. Tess removed the bric-à-brac off the mantlepiece shelves and wrapped each item in tissue. Brenda released all the clothes from the wardrobe and layered them across my bed. Aunt Margaret made a list. Then silently, slowly, the aunties and Mother folded each item back into itself and arranged them into the open cases.

Dora asked if Giovanna was going home to her parents now and Mother shook her head. Then Dora started to cry and asked where was she going then – if not home?

Brenda said, 'She'll be going where they know how to take care of her.'

But she never said who *they* were.

PETER FALLON

Late Sentinels

How would they know whether
they're coming or going
as they swish that way and this
in such fierce weather,

these winter trees between
the window and the lake,
those snappy ashes
and that steadfast evergreen,

its ivy clinging on for life?
The tips of Sitka spruces bend
like sailboats in a storm at sea.
Sturdy sceptres, emblems of strife.

Shrubs stand unshaken in the shelter
of an alcove, under eaves.
Late sentinels – their woodland
cousins flurry in a welter

of distress as when in fright
we start awake and worry
where we are. We scan the map
by lightning's light.

And so to whom now will we turn,
now that the long nights
lean on us? Now who
or what will guide us as they burn,

those fires of house and hearth,
in guttery flickers?
As if there were no end to plenty
we plundered earth.

Where are they now, those chaste priestesses
who tended embers borne from Troy
and kept them lighted year on year
for centuries? For anyone who transgresses

nothing worse than the shame –
not even the mandatory sentence,
for that became our task and duty.
We had their trust. They held us as the keepers of the flame.

GERARD FANNING

Some Stray Cuts

Let us sleepwalk or we would see the grass grow,
hear the heartbeat of the pygmy shrew,
die of the roar that lies on the other side of silence.

⁓

There is no true remembrance of former things
as there will be no remembrance of things that are to come.
All we have is our sweet *now*, musician's phrasing.

⁓

Who doesn't nip out to the corner shop
and imagine himself free, up to no good, putting
the terrible business of liver and spleen to one side?

⁓

I listen to the breeze trembling the sash windows,
memory hauling on its gears as the night barely darkens:
when all else has yielded up, the horizon glows.

⁓

What shapes are these, the clumsy architecture of fields,
monasteries, asylums, the far-off surf
of the motorway hovering at the margin of belief?

⁓

Lovers sprawled on mattresses in a backyard festooned
with creepers, unable to go back into the house
where light glows from kitchen and porch.

⊸

A car abandoned in a mid-western town, doors wide open,
a woman brings her infants at 2 am to a lonely beach,
past garden hedging planted years ago from stray cuts.

⊸

All day we smell the fires, the tossed dice of blown gravel.
The summerhouse we'd taken for July
was tucked on the heel of a soon-to-be famous promontory.

⊸

Sorrowful waders feed on gravel worms
and the Nanny's pulse scribbles data, a familiar squall
rising like an Ava Maria and lasting just about as long.

GABRIEL FITZMAURICE

Spring

After last night's thunder comes the rain,
The fertile rain from which new life will grow,
Things that were will spring to life again,
Brigid comes with seed and plough and hoe.
Past is past, let spring undo its chain,
Past is past, it's time to let it go:
Out of the long winter of our pain
Buds of spring unfold in each hedgerow.
Out of every ditch and dyke and drain
Brigid comes though harsh winds still may blow,
We yoke our horses, see them take the strain:
At one again with seed and soil, we know
That after last night's thunder comes the rain,
Things that were will spring to life again.

*Brigid: the Celtic goddess of fire, the hearth and poetry later Christianized as
Saint Brigid whose feast day is February 1st, the first day of spring.*

MIRIAM GAMBLE

An Emblem Thereof

Like Neanderthal man in his cairn
I have found myself here, face to the wall,
curled underneath the bounty of a duvet
which, though reeking of sex,
has been dubbed both a burial shroud and a caul.

How they weep, and tear at their hair!
How I hold fire, obstinately foetal.
They try the gods, but their prayers sway
weakly on the wind – they know this is no hex –
retreat into their mouths again, irresolute and fatal.

And sure enough, the word comes down
and in doing so confirms their worst suspicions:
Sorry folks; the next move is her own ...

A civil war starts over who invented manumission.
It lasts x years, during which time I stay
in the duvet, scan Proust, cultivate the wax in my ears.

ANTHONY GLAVIN

from The Notebook of Maeve Maguire

I THOUGHT I'D STOPPED writing in this notebook two months ago – until I dreamt of my mother and that crow last night. Only this time Ma actually managed to stitch its belly up, using that thick waxy thread you get for mending carpets. And it's that dream which has brought me back to this notebook one last time.

Here I sit in my Dublin kitchen, a woman of thirty-eight, still dreaming of her mother. Still working the shuttle of memory back and forth across the Big Pond as Pops always called it, from Ireland to Boston where the story begins. And back and forth and back again.

It's Christmas next week, and I've the tree up already. A surprise for Katy when she gets home from school, after which we'll trim it together, as we always do. I only strung the lights this afternoon, to see which bulbs have given up the ghost of Christmas past. It gets dark early now, so I drew the sitting-room curtains before plugging them in. Yet when I did, and it all came to life, I suddenly recalled another tree. On Christmas Eve when I was five or six, and sick to my stomach from a tummy bug, if not all the excitement. Ma put a damp face-cloth over my brow and made me lie on the sofa in our living room, opposite the Boston Common with its own coloured Christmas lights and life-sized crib. As I lay there in the dark beside our lit-up tree, I could hear Ma in the kitchen, making the shrimp & rice dish she always served on Christmas Eve, and which I never ate. It's a mellower memory than others that follow here, but I'm happy to have retrieved it.

Nor am I making it up – even if mother is the necessity of invention. Both the lies we tell our mothers, and the world we create as a counter to them. Only I'm getting ahead of myself, for had I known this much to start, I might've developed a Personality as a child. Gone on to become a weather presenter or chat-show host. Or – who knows – a writer, now that I've scribbled a book-length script? Or I might have left Boston for Barcelona or *bella Roma* instead of dirty ol' Dublin a dozen years ago. At the very least – had I known this much last year – I wouldn't have sought out Sister Una. Nor begun this notebook whose Afterword I suppose these final lines are.

It seems so obvious now – the way a truth is so often obvious – once uncovered. Out of sight under your nose, until suddenly you look down and see it. Like the truths that are buried back there in childhood: out of sight but not out of mind or memory – provided you know how to read them. How to reassemble the pictures until there's narrative enough to set you free. Or, if not entirely free, more fully back into the Here & Now – at least better positioned to get on with it.

Certainly it's taken me this long to see how large a part your mother plays in it all. Even with the help of Constance Fitzgerald, chanting that truth like a one-woman Greek chorus at work these past four years. Constance being one of forty-odd residents at the Fairview Home for the Elderly in Dublin, and Constance at seventy-eight among the oddest. Constance who is always at the front door, asking to be let out so she can go home to take care of the mother she buried in Galway over twenty years ago.

'Nurse, will you let me out? My mother's not well.'

'I haven't a key, Constance,' Assistant Matron Mary O'Mara tells her.

'Nurse, will you let me out? My mother's expecting me.'

'I'm only junior staff, Constance,' Fiona Flynn, my other Assistant Matron, fibs. 'They don't give the likes of me a key.'

'Sure, what good's a key to anyone?' says Constance, trudging slowly back to her chair in the front day-room. I used to tell Constance I wasn't trusted with a key either, but I stopped that two years ago when I became Matron. Addled as she is, Constance still knows that I'm Nurse Ratchett – the one with the big ring of keys, so to speak. It's funny how the mind works, even for those who seem parked permanently in cloud-cuckoo land. You think a resident is totally out of it, until suddenly they tune back in, like the perfect reception you sometimes get on a bockety old radio in between all the static. And you can get caught out then – if you're not careful with the lies you tell. For old folks are a lot like children if they catch you dissembling – disposed to dig in or rear up on you. Get muleish or go bolshy. Or ballistic, like Agnes Dunne does, if she thinks you're having her on. 'Germany Calling' as Mary O'Mara dubbed poor Agnes, with her head full of bombs and plots. So honesty is the best insurance policy – at least some of the time.

Of course, there are those like Larry Ferguson whose wireless only pulls in outer space. Tell Larry the world is ending tomorrow, and he'd just fix you with his impossibly bright eyes, like a squirrel on drugs, and ask for seconds of ice cream. Larry thinks the Home is some 24/7 party he's at, and he's forever asking his visitors, his granddaughters say, or even the staff, for the lend of a fiver so as to get a few drinks. 'He's the original Happy as Larry,' Mary O'Mara laughed her first week at work, and didn't 'Happy-As' stick, too. Larry's not bothered about getting out the front door, but we keep an eye on him still, as he has a habit, on days when he's feeling partied out, of walking about with his penis outside his pants. Another of the forty-odd, without a doubt about it. 'It's not the one way we all go,' as Pops used to say.

Still, it was Constance Fitzgerald who kept on like a chorus I couldn't hear, chanting her mantra about her *mater*. 'I need to go now; my mother needs me.' Most of the residents look the part – that is, clearly *not* going anywhere, God love them. But Constance looks well yet, hair neatly brushed, her cardigan generally clean. Last year a deliveryman who mistook her for a visitor took the key from behind the potted geranium at reception and opened the front door, wishing her mother a speedy recovery. That his own granny must have lived to 150 was all I could think, the fecking eejit. Though he took off after her once he realised his error, along with Polish Petra, one of our care attendants, who glimpsed Constance out front, thank God, and also went after her like a shot.

Her own mother too lies at the heart of it – yet even as Constance acted it out, I failed to cop it for myself. Constance with a shawl under her arm – for her mother who's complaining of a chill. Or wrapping a couple of biscuits in a serviette from the afternoon tea trolley: vanilla cremes, her mother's favourites. I merely figured Constance for the youngest daughter on whom it fell to care for an ageing mother, and who consequently never got to marry or raise a family of her own. Or so I assumed until a few months ago, when her nephew set us straight. Constance was the youngest, true enough, but it wasn't her mother she had handed her life over to. Which makes such invention around her mother all the more imaginative, because all the more necessary. Not to mention sad.

But I didn't understand that straight off. Nor could I yet read Constance and her confabulations as a perfect example of how we weave our own lives against the weft of our mother's. Certainly I didn't know that about myself and Mam – not in any clear sense yet. Indeed I didn't know that at all.

II

ALL I KNEW, following Pops' death September before last, was how low I was. Lower than low. Not initially – at the news of his death or the busyness of the burial – but in the months that followed. What the textbooks call 'the anguish, disorganisation and despair stage of grieving' that followed upon that early Saturday-morning phone call from my brother.

'Maeve, it's Brian.'

'Brian – what is it?' As if I couldn't already guess what had him calling at 2.00 a.m. Boston time.

'It's Pops, Maeve.'

I hate the phone at the best of times – which obviously this wasn't. Brian isn't any better on it either, and so he rang off after saying Pops had died quietly in his sleep at the nursing home, telling me to ring back when I had my flight details. I just stood there with the phone in my hand, feeling as if my life had suddenly shattered like a mirror, all bits of glass on the kitchen floor. I began to cry then – quietly – for Katy was still asleep upstairs, and I've always hated breaking down around her – as if determined to spare her the burden of a mother's unhappiness.

It was a lovely early autumn morning, better than much of the summer, with the kitchen door ajar onto the garden, where Nibbles lay sunning himself atop the coal-bunker. Inside, a wasp buzzed at the window over the sink: what we call a yellow jacket back in Boston. As I stared at the Bank of Ireland calendar on the wall, I suddenly realised it was Labor Day weekend back home. And as suddenly, the fact that Pops had died on that holiday – Pops who never stopped working – seemed utterly, cruelly apt. With that, it all came loose deep down inside, making me pitch forward. And when Katy, hearing me, came downstairs to hold me, there was nothing I could do, only put my arms around her too.

I rang Orla then, who promptly offered to stay with Katy while I flew over. I sometimes think how I'd never have survived here without Orla, and that Saturday was no exception. She came straight over too, taking a tin of Tasty Treats for Nibbles from her overnight bag, and making a big show of presenting it to K who absolutely dotes on the cat, and is mad about Orla as well.

I wanted to ring Aer Lingus when Orla came, but she made me sit and talk about Pops instead. What I said didn't make much sense – talking about the battered fedora he always wore, or his Boston Red Sox cap in summer – while Orla made me a cup of tea and Katy got her breakfast, having given Nibbles his. And when

I finally rang the airline, it was Orla who reminded me to ask for a compassionate fare, something I'd not have thought of myself.

I went down to the Home that afternoon where, as luck had it, Mary O'Mara was the weekend charge-nurse. 'Don't bother coming down,' Mary had said on the phone, saying she'd change her own roster through the week so as to keep an eye on the day-shift until I got back. But I wanted to look over the roster myself, check a few med charts, and see what else might need looking after before I flew out. And, sure enough, Constance Fitzgerald was at the front door as I came in, saying she needed to take her mother shopping. It was my father I had just lost, however, so I didn't hear what Constance was telling me. 'See if there's anything she'll watch on telly?' I suggested instead to care assistant Polish Petra, who was also working that Saturday.

Mary O'Mara had already anticipated all I'd come down to do, so I hadn't to stay long. Even so, Mary didn't start with care plans or purchase orders – all that busyness of denial I had summoned for myself. Instead she put her arms around me, giving me a moment in which to move beyond my disbelief. I've only known Mary two years, but she's nearly as big in my life as Orla is. Deep is what Mary is, and she didn't bother saying much in the office, just rubbed my back as she held me.

Constance was at the front door again as I came out of the office, so I took her in the elevator down to the newer day-room where she rarely sits, figuring the change might help settle her. As I seated her there, the Noticeboard on the wall opposite the TV caught my eye. The Noticeboard being a large white Formica board designed to help the residents keep track of a few basic facts, like the date and season, written up with a grease pencil. It also used to give 'Today's Menu' until we decided that info just gave a head start to those clients who like to grumble about the food. Its 'Thought for the Day' is the previous Matron's idea, after she found *A Book of 1000 Inspirations* at a sale of work. But most of those are saccharine enough that I keep an eye out for better stuff

– like song lyrics, a line of poetry, or even an exceptional Chinese-cookie fortune. However, there was nothing exceptional on the board this morning:

DATE: Saturday, 5th September 1990
SEASON: Autumn
WEATHER: Bright & Cool
ACTIVITY: Exercise to music
SONG FOR THE DAY: *Try to Remember the Kind of September*

Nothing out of the ordinary – which is what gave me pause. Nothing to mark this as the day my father died, back in Boston where we call autumn fall. Leaving the day-room, I went through the diningroom into the kitchen before going back upstairs. Mary O'Mara had said nothing to any of the staff, so I was able to take a quick look around without having to deal with condolences. Just long enough to see refrigerators and freezer were amply stocked, and all of Happy-As safely tucked inside his trousers.

EAMON GRENNAN

Elemental

The dream all water, a voyage
to God knows where, a setting off
through bars of this bright-mullioned window
beyond which twinkles a melange
of rush-hour traffic, yapping geese, tattered sky.

This morning after, then, you catch sight of –
rising out of muddy water –
a mud-coloured heron lifting itself
out of two elements and vaulting broad-winged
into a third, leaving a little sign
of the fire that feeds it
in the gleam of steam its breath had been.

What you wish for, watching,
is a life so right among the elements:
to be there in that perfect present
absolute, be a self flung headlong
into the future, past looking back –
simply becoming the world as it becomes you,
becomes whatever's been brought
to this moment as it is
on extended wing: a balance happening.

Parking Lot with Pigeons

Glittering they rise in a curlicue of luminous grey
under light rain that turns the concrete lot to a glaze

of broken illuminations, each lasting a moment only
as one car then another splashes through its reflection

to send short-lived sprays of radiance up as the birds twist
and soar, bank, glide back down to settle, twitching a little

their inches of iridescence, and forming with no intent at all
a shape that won't be still, shifting every which way, letting

anything be the case. But from where you've stopped to watch
you see it shape its own pattern that's open to anything

that is the case, that might take place: no exercise
of special power, no grand design invoked, intended,

but all at its kinetic ease, so from any angle you could say
That's right!, seeing the rainbow where spilt petrol spreads.

VONA GROARKE

The Recital

Beads from a necklace
dropped on black tiles

while the choir
chainlinks
blue enamel and gilt

are no more
disturbance than

sunlight piercing
at right angles
stained glass.

KERRY HARDIE

Dutchmen's Trousers
i.m. my mother-in-law, Shelagh Hardie 1912 -1995

She'd search the wide sky for a break in the cloud,
some rent in the grey expanse.
'There,' she would tell me, 'just enough blue
to make a Dutchman his trousers.'

All afternoon it promised more rain,
then colour blew in from the back of the sea,
and I knew she was up in the sky with the wind,
wrenching the storm-clouds apart.

I was wearing no shoes, I had to take care
because of the sea holly, sharp in the dunes,
though not the late heartsease, purple and yellow,
those colours the skin takes from bruising.

The sea holly's leaves are the washed jade of water,
its spikes are as long and relentless as grief,
its blooms are the blue of the cloth that they used
for those story-book, baggy Dutch trousers.

Heartsease is the herbalist's name for wild pansies,
which she never trusted – their bright, clever faces –
she tried not to look too hard at the world,
at the people with thorns in their eyes.

But heartsease has petals as soft as fine silk,
and ragged blue trousers come patched with grey sky,
and needles of sea-holly sew a deep seam
through the dunes and the wave-wash of lace.

JAMES HARPUR

Angels and Harvesters

As thoughts arrive
From god knows where,
Or sun breaks through
A fraying cloud
Emboldening a patch
Of trees, or grass,
They just appeared
From nowhere
Among the harvesters
The field a world
Of cutting, gathering,
Cutting, gathering.
Their outlines sometimes
Flickering brighter,
They walked between
The bending figures
Curious
Pausing to watch,
Like ancestors
Almost remembering
The world they'd left,
Or foreigners
Amused to see
The same things done.
They moved around
Unseen by all –
Unless one glimpsed,
Perhaps, light thicken,
A glassy movement,

As air can wobble
On summer days.
And then they went
Walked into nothing
Just left the world
Without ceremony
Unless it was
The swish of scythes
The swish of scythes.

JACK HARTE

Lofty learns the Business
An Excerpt from the novel 'Reflections in a Tar-Barrel'

'Reflections in a Tar-Barrel' deals with the trials, tribulations, and escapades of a character called Lofty, who is a supposed half-wit but really has just a minor cognitive problem which has been exacerbated by both school and family attitude. When he is apprenticed to a hawker of religious goods, he finally begins to learn and gain confidence. – JH

H E SEEMED CONTENT to be passing on his knowledge and experience to me. Strange really. On the other hand, maybe not. I was the only one he had to take over from him at the end of his days. But, I suppose, the way he looked at it, better a half-wit than nobody. Better that than having to drive the van into a ditch and leave it there to rust into the earth.

It must have seemed a daunting task when he saw my first efforts. But he was so cool-headed. So totally relaxed. Whenever I expected him to get frustrated, or excited, or annoyed, it never happened. He would take out his pipe and slowly light it. By the time he had completed that operation he would be ready to re-focus his attention and deal with the crisis.

He tried to teach me the same technique. Keeping cool, that is.

'Listen, son,' he said to me after he had been observing me for a few days. 'Anyone can see you have a problem. There's no denying you have a problem. But it's only a problem. It's not the end of the world. What we've got to do is identify what the problem is and then find a way of solving it or else a way of getting around it. My opinion is that you are far too excitable. You get worked up about everything. If an old lady comes up to the stall to buy a statue of the Sacred Heart from you, that is a transaction, not a blooming crisis. So there is no need to get excited. No need to pump every ounce of blood from your toes up into your face. No need to blow fuses all over the place. The old lady is a customer, that's all. She does not see you as a person. She doesn't think of you as a person. She is not wondering whether you are happy or sad, whether you are carefree or laden down with the worries of the world. She wants a statue of the Sacred Heart, and she wants to give you the money. That's the height of it. So you've got to detach yourself. You've got to find the switches inside you and learn to switch on the brain and switch off the feelings. Then you'll be able to think with your brain alone, and not with your belly or your heart.'

You know, that made sense to me. It was the first time in my life I got a bit of advice that actually made sense. And I began to work on it. I began to develop little techniques for staying cool. Detached. I would say, over and over, to myself: these are customers, not people. All they want from me is to be served. They don't know me. I don't know them. They are not interested in me, and I don't give a fiddler's curse about them. And it slowly began to have an effect. Whenever there was a problem, or someone asked me a question I could not answer immediately, I tried to use his trick of taking a couple of steps back in rapt concentration, working out the response, and then turning back to the customer. But I couldn't manage it. I was too static. Like it or not, I was rooted to the ground, staring at the customer, mouth open, no doubt. However, in my mind I followed his procedure. Switched off, thought about the problem, worked out the answer, then came back to the customer, so to speak.

He should have been a teacher. Stephen Hanlon. He had that kind of way with him. He would show me how to do something. Demonstrate it. Then invite me to have a go. Say, erecting the bars for the stall and pinning the canvas around it. When I got stuck, as I always did in the early days, he would step in. First of all he would point out how much I had got right. Focus on that first. Then, with my confidence boosted, he would show me where I had gone astray, and how to proceed. All of this in his calm and calming manner. Yes, Stephen should have been a teacher. He was great.

Soon I was harder to overawe. Guided by his gentle nudges, grunts, and nods, I began to learn the business. How to pack and unpack the stock. How to set up the stall from the back of the van. How to lay out the display of items so that people would see each one clearly.

'That's good, son, but do you think the rosary beads would look better hanging up somewhere?' he would ask in slow earnestness. And of course when I searched, I would discover there was a hook attached to an overhead bar perfectly placed for the hanging of rosary beads.

I loved the way he called me 'son'. It wasn't exactly a term of affection with him, but it wasn't patronising either. And it sounded so appropriate from him because of his age. He must have been seventy, but he was a very fresh seventy. Slight of build. Clear skin. White hair, but no sign of balding. He wore clothes more appropriate to a younger man. A short tweed overcoat, navy blue. Trousers that were cut slim on the legs. A soft hat, tweed, with a little feather in the band of it. And of course the pipe. Always there or thereabouts. If he wasn't smoking it, he was cleaning it out, or priming it with fresh tobacco. He used a brand called Clan, already flaked, which came in a green packet with a tartan design.

He called me 'son' and it seemed genuine, seemed to signify a bond between us. Which astonished me. I'm not saying I felt disowned by everyone else in the whole world. Not altogether disowned. The range of people's attitudes would have gone from cold contempt, in my mother's case, to indifference, in the case of most people, to a kind of warm acceptance by my cousins and all the old people I visited. The only person I ever felt really close to was my father. At least that's my memory of our brief relationship. But I was a child then, his child, so that was different. Now, here I was at eighteen, awkward and ugly, couldn't read nor write, couldn't put two words together towards a conversation, and yet this old man seemed to like me, seemed to have adopted me.

It was just as well he felt positive towards me, because he had to teach me the business one way or the other. My lack of the skills I should have picked up in school were the next obstacle.

'I've been watching you, son, and you get into a hell of a fluster whenever a person wants to buy more than one thing. You mustn't be too good at the old addition.'

'No,' I grunted.

'Yet, you know the price of everything. I'm amazed how smartly you picked up the prices.'

'I'm good at remembering.'

'Are you now?' he laughed. 'Why don't we try you out then? We'll change the prices on a dozen items. I'll write them down as I call them out, and we'll see how many you can remember.'

He took out his notebook and the little pencil that was sheathed in the spine. 'Now,' he said, and began to rattle off items from the stall, putting new prices on each one.

I concentrated, because I liked to impress him, and this was child's play to me. Concentrated on his voice. Registered it on my ear.

When he had finished, he paused. 'Now, are you ready?'

I nodded. He called out items at random and I put a price on them. I could see him ticking them off as he called them out. When he called out the last one he lowered the notebook and looked at me. I gave him my answer.

'Bloody amazing,' he said. 'Every single one right. There's no one else that I know of who could do that. That's brilliant. Now, will we try out the additions?'

'Alright.' I was delighted he had been impressed with my feat of memory, but I braced myself for the imminent fall.

'A customer buys two items costing seventeen pence and twenty-eight pence. How much does he owe you?'

I struggled hard with the sum but could make no headway.

'How much is eight and seven?' he prompted me.

'Fifteen.'

'How do you know that?'

'I learned my tables in school.' Yes, learning tables had never been a problem. I learned then to the point of boredom, while listening to other children reciting theirs.

'If you know your tables, you should be able to add. Try this out. Make a picture in your head of a sheet of white paper. Right? Now put down twenty-eight on that piece of paper. Right? Underneath that put seventeen. Right? Draw a line. Now add it up the way you would on a real sheet of paper.'

I tried. Tried hard. But the figures on the piece of paper kept floating around and fading away. Like those magic notepads from Woolworths from which the writing disappears as soon as you bend it. I wrote down the figures again, tried to concentrate more intensely on them, twenty-eight, seventeen, but, as soon as I went to write an answer down, the original figures floated off the page.

Not that I would have been any better with an actual sheet of paper. Moments like these I grew impatient with him. Wanted to shout, Look, I'm thick, can you not see that? Ask anyone. They'll tell you how thick I am. Frigging quick they'll tell you, with a hundred stories to prove the point.

But Stephen Hanlon was not one who let other people do his thinking for him. A problem was a problem until a solution was found. Or a way around the problem. A few days later he turned up with a calculator, the first I had ever seen.

'I think this might be the answer, son. You're a wizard at remembering prices. So all you have to do is clock them in here like this. Press the button here to add them up. Now if somebody gives you a bigger amount, and you have to subtract what he owes you, clock this in as well. Press this subtract button, and, would you believe, there's the change you have to give him.'

I couldn't believe it. A gadget to do all the things I could never manage. I took it from him as if it was gold, as if it was so fragile it might disintegrate in my hands. I felt like kneeling before the ingenuity of it. No mirage either. There it was. In my hands. A gadget. To add and subtract. Nothing could get the better of me anymore. With this gadget I could conquer the world.

I loved the business. I loved those plaster statues, those crucifixes, those rosary beads and scapulars. I loved them all. Laid them out with loving care. Took pride in knowing where to buy them wholesale, at what price. Knowing where they were manufactured. Italy mostly.

But the real ecstasy was in learning to drive the van. It was bliss even to sit in the cab. The upholstery worn away. Coming apart at the seams. The stuffed fibre peeping out. When my Aunt Brigid looked inside one day and noticed this, she threatened to crochet a set of seat covers. I hoped fervently she would forget about this. I preferred it the way it was. More manly. Coarse. In keeping with the used appearance of the van itself. Definitely no crocheted coverings. Yes, the rest of the cab was in character with the tattered upholstery. The paint on the dash was chipped off on protruding surfaces. The glass lens of the fuel gauge was cracked. Far from being blemishes, these were beauty spots to me. I could scarcely wait until the van was mine. Totally mine.

Driving along to a fair or a mission, Stephen used the time to train me. Always used the time.

'Now, son, get out the calculator. Mrs Murphy has come into some money, twenty pounds that her sister sent her from the States for her birthday. She is a very religious woman, Mrs Murphy, and she comes to your stall to buy presents for the whole family.'

'Good old Mrs Murphy,' I chirped in approval, as I set up the calculator on my knees.

'Now, she buys two miraculous medals on silver chains for Molly and Mary, the twins, at seventy-five pence each, a new rosary beads for himself at one twenty-five – he has the old one worn down to the chain praying for whatever nag he puts a few bob on out of his pension money every Friday – a mass card at sixty pence to send back to her sister, Dolly, in the States, after she has it signed by Father Dempsey himself, of course, a statue of the Child of Prague for the sitting-room to replace the one with the broken head that himself knocked down last Patrick's Day when he came staggering home from the pub, that's a big investment at four seventy five, and she almost forgot, another mass card for her cousin's anniversary that's coming up in a fortnight's time.'

'Nothing like buying in time,' I chirped.

'You pack that lot into the big shopping bag that she brought with her. She hands you her twenty quid. How much change will you give her?'

Tapping away on the calculator ignoring his deliberate rambling distractions, I reply confidently: 'Her bill is eight seventy. She gives me twenty, so I give her back eleven thirty.'

'Correct.'

'Yahoo.' I yelled in triumph.

'You'll have no bother,' said Stephen. 'No bother at all. If you can get that brain of yours working, there will be no stopping you. You remind me of one time I called to a house of certain friends of mine. When I sat down, the woman of the house put on the kettle, and asked me would I have an egg. I said I would. Over she went to this sparkling new washing machine that was standing in the corner, opened the lid, and took out an egg. I started laughing and said it was a strange place to keep her eggs. "I might as well make some use of it," says she. "John in America sent over the money for it to Murrays' shop and they landed it up, as a surprise. John remembered how much scrubbing I did on the clothes every Monday and he thought that this machine would do the scrubbing for me. But I have been trying to figure out how it works, and the devil damn me, but I can't make head nor tail of it." "Did they give you a manual, a book of instructions?" said I. "They did," said she, taking it down from the dresser and putting it on the table in front of me. "See if you can figure it out." I started reading the manual and went over to look at the machine. There was something odd about it alright. Then I twigged it. It was the wrong manual. They had given her the instructions for a different model altogether. And do you know what I think? I think schools are a bit like that. They have one manual, one set of instructions, and a whole range of different models in front of them. And I'll tell you what, son, you were one of the models that didn't match their set of instructions. That's the only reason you got left behind. That's why you can't read nor write. So if you'll take my advice, you'll search for the right set of instructions and start all over again trying to get that old washing machine of yours working. In the mean time every night you should kneel down beside your bed and say three times, "I am not thick, just different." Will you do that, son? And now it's time you took a little turn at the wheel.'

And he halted on a stretch of open road. He got out slowly, walked around to the passenger door, while I clambered into the driving seat, my head full of wild possibilities, pincered between ecstatic excitement and terrified trepidation.

DERMOT HEALY

The Travels of Sorrow

for the Mac Sweeneys

Years ago, one of the two
Brothers, Pat Donlon,

Who did the cooking in the house
In a long apron to below the knee,

Went into a rage
And took the china

In the house –
The flower vase

The milk jug
The big plates –

And threw them
Onto the rocks

On the beach.
Years later,

As I built up
A wall of stone

Against the sea
I began to find

Here, a handle,
There, a small flower

Set in delph.
And they were all

The one style
Of porcelain

That came with the house.
A thousand thousand

High tides
Have been and gone

And,
With a terrible sadness,

These broken remains
Of an old argument on the alt

Are coming in amongst
The gravel,

Petals from the dresser
And the mantelpiece,

The little fractures
Of despair –

Shouting *I've had enough!*
Take it, take it all! –

Are gathering
In the surf.

For years they've been going in
And out with the tide.

Sorrow never travels
Far from home.

Xmas 2006

MICHAEL D. HIGGINS

No More Than That

Now ebbs the tide
Leaving
Strewn in a chaos of surprise
Disjointed weeds
Clinging to life
Some way to lifeless sand.

The casual gaze
Is on the bits and pieces
Left lingering
Suggesting a search
For a story abandoned
To a restless tide.

On the last ebb tide
The soul will leave
Or is it just a conceit
To hope
For a return
To some ancient embrace?

In land-locked reason
We make our endings
Bits and pieces
Without a story,
No more than that.

RITA ANN HIGGINS

Nearly Falling

In the TB ward
on Christmas day
we settled down
for 'telly time'.

Delia said over and over,
Charlie Charlie, chap chap chap.
How can he be on telly
when he's a dead duck?

We kept watching the telly.
Delia kept up her rant.

One of the patients said,
shuussssh Delia.
Then we all started.
Yeah Delia,
shut the fuck up.

Don't you shuussssh me
you streals of misery
with sputum mugs to match,
I've seen better looking bodies
on half-eaten crows.

You're watching a dead man dancing
waddling on the soles of his feet,
nearly falling and not falling.
And you don't see anything wrong with that!

You sit there;
Mary Melanchollies
your jelly babies
your blankety blank eyes
your jam jaws.

Chaste

Your whip tongue,
a bull's eye.
I limp away.

Later you slip
a three-penny bit
under my pillow.

I open one bruised heart.

FRED JOHNSTON

Tell Me Where It Hurts

Is *this* sore?
Professional fingers prod, and I say no.
And here?
Yes. A little.
Can you turn your head?
No. Hardly.

He produces a plastic vertebrae
and explains: a disk, a nerve, pain.
A few days, he says, and you'll be fine.

No, I won't, of course.
Thirty years ago he could have fobbed
me off with that, but I know better –
the pain is caused by brakes being applied,
things that can't be oiled any more
that don't run smoothly.

You ask me why I am depressed,
and I say: *I know how it will begin,*
with someone saying in a few days you'll
be rightly
and I knowing better.

Circular

We went about in circles
one hand on the next man's shoulders
something out of Gogol or Great War blind:
we had chicken soup,
which didn't agree with everybody,
it gave one old man bad stomach cramps:
he was taken away, snotting.

A trustee, if such a thing were
imaginable in a lunatic asylum, clicked
around as part of a service-trolley,
selling cigarettes
and bars of chocolate
but never newspapers; no telling
what bad news could do to the mind.

My wife arrived to say
she had custody of our children;
it was no surprise, we wept dutifully
and she left, a slim woman
working the buttons
on the door's keypad expertly –
others, receiving similar news, screamed.

Some couldn't face crossing the road,
their first day out alone:
they stood like skittles on the edge
of movement, tottering, jigging –
one by one they'd laugh or cry
and huddle back to safety along the hedge
that hid our stately windows and our tidy rooms.

CLAIRE KEEGAN

The Parting Gift

W HEN SUNLIGHT REACHES the foot of the dressing table,
you get up and look through the suitcase again. It's
hot in New York but it may turn cold in winter. All
morning the bantam cocks have crowed. It's not something you
will miss. You must dress and wash, polish your shoes. Outside,
dew lies on the fields, white and blank as pages. Soon the sun will
burn it off. It's a fine day for the hay.

In her bedroom your mother is moving things around, opening
and closing doors. You wonder what it will be like for her when
you leave. Part of you doesn't care. She talks through the door.

'You'll have a boiled egg?'

'No thanks, Ma.'

'You'll have something?'

'Later on, maybe.'

'I'll put one on for you.'

Downstairs, water spills into the kettle, the bolt slides back.
You hear the dogs rush in, the shutters folding. You've always
preferred this house in summer: cool feeling in the kitchen, the
back door open, scent of the dark wallflowers after rain.

In the bathroom you brush your teeth. The screws in the
mirror have rusted, and the glass is cloudy. You look at yourself
and know you have failed the Leaving Cert. The last exam was
history and you blanked out on the dates. You confused the
methods of warfare, the kings. English was worse. You tried to
explain that line about the dancer and the dance.

You go back to the bedroom and take out the passport. You
look strange in the photograph, lost. The ticket says you will arrive
in Kennedy Airport at 12.25, much the same time as you leave.
You take one last look around the room: walls papered yellow with

roses, high ceiling stained where the slate came off, cord of the electric heater swinging out like a tail from under the bed. It used to be an open room at the top of the stairs but Eugene put an end to all of that, got the carpenters in and the partition built, installed the door. You remember him giving you the key, how much that meant to you at the time.

Downstairs, your mother stands over the gas cooker waiting for the pot to boil. You stand at the door and look out. It hasn't rained for days; the spout that runs down from the yard is little more than a trickle. The scent of hay drifts up from neighbouring fields. As soon as the dew burns it off, the Rudd brothers will be out in the meadows turning the rows, saving it while the weather lasts. With pitchforks they'll gather what the baler leaves behind. Mrs Rudd will bring out the flask, the salad. They will lean against the bales and eat their fill. Laughter will carry up the avenue, clear, like birdcall over water.

'It's another fine day.' You feel the need for speech.

Your mother makes some animal sound in her throat. You turn to look at her. She wipes her eyes with the back of her hand. She's never made any allowance for tears.

'Is Eugene up?' she says.

'I don't know. I didn't hear him.'

'I'll go and wake him.'

It's going on for six. Still an hour before you leave. The saucepan boils and you go over to lower the flame. Inside, three eggs knock against each other. One is cracked, a ribbon streaming white. You turn down the gas. You don't like yours soft.

Eugene comes down wearing his Sunday clothes. He looks tired. He looks much the same as he always does.

'Well, Sis,' he says. 'Are you all set?'

'Yeah.'

'You have your ticket and everything?'

'I do.'

Your mother puts out the cups and plates, slices a quarter out of the loaf. This knife is old, its teeth worn in places. You eat the bread, drink the tea and wonder what Americans eat for breakfast. Eugene tops his egg, butters bread, shares it with the dogs. Nobody says anything. When the clock strikes six, Eugene reaches for his cap.

'There's a couple of things I've to do up the yard,' he says. 'I won't be long.'

'That's all right.'

'You'd want to leave on time,' your mother says. 'You wouldn't want to get a puncture.'

You place your dirty dishes on the draining board. You have nothing to say to your mother. If you started, you would say the wrong things and you wouldn't want it to end that way. You go upstairs but you'd rather not go back into the room. You stand on the landing. They start talking in the kitchen but you don't hear what they say. A sparrow swoops down onto the window ledge and pecks at his reflection, his beak striking the glass. You watch him until you can't watch him any longer and he flies away.

⁓

Your mother didn't want a big family. Sometimes, when she lost her temper, she told you she would put you in a bucket, and drown you. As a child you imagined being taken by force to the edge of the Slaney River, being placed in a bucket, and the bucket being flung out from the bank, floating for a while before it sank. As you grew older you knew it was only a figure of speech, and then you believed it was just an awful thing to say. People sometimes said awful things.

Your eldest sister was sent off to the finest boarding school in Ireland, and became a school teacher. Eugene was gifted in school but when he turned fourteen your father pulled him out to work the land. In the photographs the eldest are dressed up: satin ribbons and short trousers, a blinding sun in their eyes. The others just came along, as nature took its course, were fed and clothed, sent off to the boarding schools. Sometimes they came back for a bank-holiday weekend. They brought gifts and an optimism that quickly waned. You could see them remembering everything, the existence, turning rigid when your father's shadow crossed the floor. Leaving, they'd feel cured, impatient to get away.

Your turn at boarding school never came. By then your father saw no point in educating girls; you'd go off and another man would have the benefit of your education. If you were sent to the day school you could help in the house, the yard. Your father moved into the other room but your mother gave him sex on his birthday. She'd go into his room and they'd have it there. It never took long and they never made noise but you knew. And then that too stopped and you were sent instead, to sleep with your father. It happened once a month or so, and always when Eugene was out.

You went willingly at first, crossed the landing in your nightdress, put your head on his arm. He played with you, praised you, told you you had the brains, that you were the brightest child. Then the terrible hand reaching down under the clothes to pull up the nightdress, the fingers, strong from milking, finding you. The mad hand going at himself until he groaned and then him asking you to reach over for the cloth, saying you could go then, if you wanted. The mandatory kiss at the end, stubble, and cigarettes on the breath. Sometimes he gave you a cigarette of your own and you could lie beside him smoking, pretending you were someone else. You'd go into the bathroom when it was over and wash, telling yourself it meant nothing, hoping the water would be hot.

Now you stand on the landing trying to remember happiness, a good day, an evening, a kind word. It seems apt to search for something happy to make the parting harder but nothing comes to mind. Instead you remember that time the setter had all those pups. It was around the same time your mother started sending you into his room. In the spout-house, your mother leant over the half barrel, and held the sack under the water until the whimpering stopped and the sack went still. That day she drowned the pups, she turned her head and looked at you, and smiled.

≈

Eugene comes up and finds you standing there.

'It doesn't matter,' he says. 'Pay no heed.'

'What doesn't matter?'

He shrugs and goes into the room he shares with your father. You drag the suitcase downstairs. Your mother hasn't washed the dishes. She is standing there at the door with a bottle of holy water. She shakes some of this water on you. Some of it gets in your eyes. Eugene comes down with the car keys.

'Da wants to talk to you.'

'He's not getting up?'

'No. You're to go up to him.'

'Go on,' Ma says. 'Don't leave empty-handed.'

You go back up the stairs, stop outside his room. You haven't gone through this door since the blood started, since you were twelve. You open it. It's dim inside, stripes of summer light around the curtains. There's that same old smell of cigarette smoke and feet. You look at his shoes and socks beside the bed. You feel sick. He sits up in his vest, the cattle dealer's eyes taking it all in, measuring.

'So you're going to America,' he says.

You say you are.

'Aren't you the sly one?' He folds the sheet over his belly. 'Will it be warm out there?'

You say it will.

'Will there be anyone to meet you?'

'Yes.' Agree with him. Always, that was your strategy.

'That's all right, so.'

You wait for him to get the wallet out or to tell you where it is, to fetch it. Instead, he puts his hand out. You don't want to touch him but maybe the money is in his hand. In desperation you extend yours, and he shakes it. He draws you towards him. He wants to kiss you. You don't have to look at him to know he's smiling. You pull away, turn out of the room but he calls you back. This is his way. He'll give it to you now that he knows you thought you'd get nothing.

'And another thing,' he says. 'Tell Eugene I want them meadows knocked by dark.'

You go out and close the door. In the bathroom you wash your hands, your face, compose yourself once more.

'I hope he gave you money?' your mother says.

'He did,' you say.

'How much did he give you?'

'A hundred pound.'

'He broke his heart,' she says. 'His own daughter, the last of ye, and he wouldn't even get out of the bed and you going to America. Wasn't it a black bastard I married!'

'Are you ready?' Eugene says. 'We better hit the road.'

You put your arms around your mother. You don't know why. She changes when you do this. You can feel her getting soft in your arms.

'I'll send word, Ma, when I get there.'

'Do,' she says.

'It'll be night before I do.'

'I know,' she says. 'The journey's long.'

Eugene takes the suitcase and you follow him outside. The cherry trees are bending. *The stronger the wind, the stronger the tree.* The sheep dogs follow you. You walk on, past the flower beds, the pear trees, on out towards the car. The Cortina is parked under the chestnut's shade. You can smell the wild mint beside the diesel tank. Eugene turns the engine and tries to make some joke, starts down the avenue. You look again at your handbag, your ticket, the passport. You will get there, you tell yourself. They will meet you.

Eugene stops in the avenue before the gates.

'Da gave you nothing, sure he didn't?'

'What?'

'I know he didn't. You needn't let on.'

'It doesn't matter.'

'All I have is a twenty-pound note. I can send you money later on.'

'It doesn't matter.'

'Do you think it would be safe to send money in the post?'

It is a startling question, stupid. You look at the gates, at the woods beyond.

'Safe?'

'Yeah.'

'Yes,' you say you think it will.

You get out and open the gates. He drives through, stops to wait for you. As you put the wire on, the filly trots down to the edge of the field, leans up against the fence, and whinnies. She's a red chestnut with one white stocking. You sold her to buy your ticket but she will not be collected until tomorrow. That was the arrangement. You watch her and turn away but it's impossible not to look back. Your eyes follow the gravel road, the strip of green between the tracks, on up to the granite post left there from Protestant days and, past it, your mother who has come out to see the last of you. She waves a cowardly little wave, and you wonder if she will ever forgive you for leaving her there with her husband.

On down the avenue, the Rudds are already in the meadows. There's a shot from an engine as something starts, a bright clap of laughter. You pass Barna Cross where you used to catch the bus to the Community School. Towards the end, you hardly bothered going. You simply sat in the wood under the trees all day or, if it was raining, you found a hayshed. Sometimes you read the books your sisters left behind. Sometimes you fell asleep. Once a man came into his hayshed and found you there. You kept your eyes closed. He stood there for a long time and then he went away.

'There's something you should know,' Eugene says.

'Oh?'

'I'm not staying.'

'What do you mean?'

'I'm giving up the land. They can keep it.'

'What?'

'Can you see me living there with them until the end of their days? Could you see me bringing a woman in? What woman could stand it? I'd have no life.'

'But what about all the work you've done, all that time?'

'I don't care about any of that,' he says. 'All that is over.'

'Where will you go?'

'I don't know. I'll rent some place.'

'Where?'

'I don't know yet. I was waiting until you left. I didn't think any further.'

'You didn't stay on my account?'

He slows the car and looks over. 'I did,' he says. 'But I wasn't much use, was I, Sis?'

It is the first time anyone has ever mentioned it. It feels like a terrible thing, being said.

'You couldn't be there all the time.'

'No,' he says. 'I suppose I couldn't.'

Between Baltinglass and Blessington the road winds. You remember this part of the road. You came this way for the All Ireland finals. Your father had a sister in Tallaght he could stay with, a hard woman who made great tarts and left a chain of smoke. Boggy fields, bad land surround this road, and a few ponies grazing. As a child, you thought this was the West of Ireland. It used to make the adults laugh, to hear you say it. And now you suddenly remember one good thing about your father. It was before you had begun to go into his room. He had gone into the village and stopped at the garage for petrol. The girl at the pumps came up to him and told him she was the brightest girl in the class, the best at every subject, until you came along. He'd come back from the village and repeated this, and he was proud because you were brighter than the Protestant's daughter.

Close to the airport, planes appear in the sky. Eugene parks the car and helps you find the desk. Neither one of you knows exactly what to do. They look at your passport, take your suitcase and tell you where to go. You step onto moving stairs that frighten you. There's a coffee shop where Eugene tries to make you eat a fry but you don't want to eat or stay and keep him company.

Your brother embraces you. You have never been embraced this way. When his stubble grazes your face, you pull back.

'I'm sorry,' he says.

'It's all right.'

'Goodbye, Sis.'

'Goodbye, Eugene. Take care.'

'Watch out for pickpockets in New York.'

You cannot answer.

'Write,' he says quickly. 'Don't forget to write.'

'I won't. Don't worry.'

You follow passengers through a queue and leave him behind. He will not go back for the fry; he hasn't the time. You did not have to deliver the message. You know he will put his boot down, be home before noon, have the meadows knocked long before dark. After that there will be corn to cut. Already the winter barley's turning. September will bring more work, old duties to the land. Sheds to clean out, cattle to test, lime to spread, dung. You know he will never leave the fields.

A stranger asks for your handbag, and you give it to him. You pass through a frame that has no door and your handbag is returned to you. On the other side, the lights are bright. There's the smell of perfume and roasted coffee beans, expensive things. You make out bottles of tanning lotion, a rack of dark glasses. It is all getting hazy but you keep on going, because you must, past the T-shirts and the duty-free towards the gate. When you find it, there is hardly anyone there but you know this is the place. You look for another door, make out part of a woman's body. You push it, and it opens. You pass bright hand-basins, mirrors. Someone asks are you all right – *such a stupid question* – but you do not cry until you have opened and closed another door, until you have safely locked yourself inside your stall.

(from *Walk the Blue Fields*, Faber and Faber, 2007)

BRENDAN KENNELLY

Fighting January

'The best way to fight the January
dark and cold,' she said,
'is to tell a few stories
that have a touch of sunlight.
If you can't do that,
take the man of your dreams to bed
and journey through him
as if he were a warm country
in an icy time.
Find the music of his body
and let your heart dance to it
with the kind of abandon you knew so well
those Sunday nights in the parish hall
when all the guys surrounded you
and you chose the lad
with the mad body
and the gentle eyes.
Not much talk out of him
but when the dance was over
he looked in your eyes and said,
"Thanks for makin' me warm in here.
'Tis fierce cold outside."'

THOMAS KINSELLA

Free Fall

I was falling, helpless in a shower of waste,
reaching my arms out toward the others
falling in disorder everywhere around me.

At the last instant,
approaching the flaming surface,
the fall was suddenly very slow.

We were unconcerned,
regarding one another in approval.

ANATOLY KUDRYAVITSKY

An Italian Rensaku

(Haiku Sequence from Tuscany and Lazio)

morning traffic
geese honk from the roof
of a *palazzo*

a grass snake
escaping into
my thought of it

beach grass
off colour …
a bright green lizard

fireflies dancing slowly
the rhythm of
a lighthouse beam

twilit ruins
a cat's shadow joins
the shadowplay

JESSIE LENDENNIE

Grattan Road

Walking here
Has become my life;
The air, the light,
Clouds like the softest
Frosted breath;
The first autumn.

I have been here
Long before the air
Smelt of change ....

And every mood
Has its vision ...
The horizon is both
This path
And the edge of the sea

And my life is bound
By every early morning,
Wanting to be here,
Wanting to be gone.

Midnight

In this New York blue-black evening
Even the rain is hollow.
No one knows me or my scribbling
Here in this smooth fluorescent nighttime
Where the lights are the lights of the half-dark
The almost dark.
I am alone with word, and almost deed.

I am fearful of how words become other things,
Hard like fluorescent red on midnight lino
Hard as anger and separation
When what I look for is the calm
Of self-involved voices.

Maybe I want to take that chance now,
Before I die alone in someone else's life
Like so many lost conversations
In midnight airports; like tickets lost and found,
Exchanged in corridors
Where I keep silent for fear of being placed
On the wrong side of midnight.

JINX LENNON

Human Dartboard

You you you, you you you, you
Are a human dartboard

You walk down the street in the 8 pm dusk
In a sweatshirt, with a circle printed on your chest,
A circle that shows at this moment in time
That you expect those around you, others around you
To treat you like you you you, you you you, you
Are a human dartboard

And in years to come you will walk upon, stand upon,
Wipe your feet on, rub your feet on
Those around you, others around you,
Cos right now you feel that you you you, you you you, you
Are a human dartboard

And when you walk back to your home
You expect no enlightenment, no encouragement
When you walk into the room on one side you see
A dull, lifeless, blood sucked-out face;
On the other side you see
A red lantern-jawed narcoleptic staring into space,
Holding something in their hand,
Something towards you, something that is bound to make
      you feel
At this moment in time that you you you, you you you, you
Are a human dartboard

And in years to come you will walk upon, stand upon,
Wipe your feet on, rub your feet on
Those around you, others around you,
Cos right now you feel that you you you, you you you, you
Are a human dartboard

And as you walk through the schools, the factories, the hospitals,
    the streets,
See the high authoritative figures that are supposed to look after
    you, take care of you
Looking through plate-glass windows, firing little triangular
    stares
Full of tiny psychic darts towards you, tiny psychic darts that are
    meant to make you feel
That at this moment in time you you you, you you you, you
Are a human dartboard

You you you, you you you, you
Are a human dartboard

DAVE LORDAN

I dream of crowds

I dream of crowds, in different guises.
I dream of drunken orgiastic crowds on sandy cliffs and beaches.
The aboriginal sun never falling. Everyone wearing the sun as a
    crown.

I dream a crowded DART, a mile-long DART
snaking through a bombed-out Cork,
past blazing stacks on Wexford hills,
through cratered Dublin exurbs

and the passengers all dressed in sackcloth rags,
a sorry exodus with overspilling suitcases
in a glazed-eye shock that seems enchantment,
squat on seatless carriages

all hypnotic concentration on
one missing infant's undulating wail
that never stops.

I dream a carnival crowd from my primary years.
Feral chaws in stripes and masks
picting through my childhood town

provoking for sport
the well-primed hate
of other, crushed inhabitants.

A part of me, a knowing part,
a mockingly prophetic part,

has yet to abandon
the animal tribe of my youth.

Then I dream an underground crowd,
an enormous underworld crowd on the march.

Their bodies are thickets of shadow,
their legs an endless Bohemian wood.

So many flushed, exhausted middle-aged faces,
grim faces of miners, musicians and executives,
sardined together there in close and hopeless darkness,
hard of breath and groaning and not even muttering
thin fibs of consolation to themselves.

Nearby, a throbbing edge is leaking to a constant flow
which might be surging hell's volcanic flood,

might be a river of decomposed sludge

or might not be an edge at all

but be the elliptical curve
where the protean crowd I don't own
with no beginning or end in my head

is alway doubling doubling doubling doubling
doubling back
upon the treadmill of itself

in the mobius way
the whitecoats say
our universe does.

AIFRIC MacAODHA

Syrinx: Tosach

Oscailt de shórt ar bith,
Ní thagann ann le nádúr.
An ghiolcach ar fás fán loch,
Do chaití í a ghearradh.

Syrinx: Opening

No opening is ever natural,
Even the reed at the water's edge
Is preparing to be gathered.

Translated by Ian Ó Caoimh

CATHERINE PHIL MacCARTHY

Irish Elk

Giant antlers shine at night
diamond, sapphire, branch

in a neighbour's garden, light
up the moonless dark

for children going to bed
as if the Irish elk,

extinct seven thousand years,
turned in his grave

beneath the lake at Lough Gur
and bellowing rose

from the bog, trailing peat
from his hinds, to roam

the hills and woods of Ireland,
ghost at large, and twice

as tall as Man, come back to
haunt us, at this time:

snow general all over
the land, he drops his

sovereign head to nibble
tufts of frozen grass.

JOHN MacKENNA

Hay-on-Wye Gravestone

> *ALSO TO THE MEMORY OF*
> *TWO SONS OF THE LATE MR. MUNN,*
> *FOR MANY YEARS NATIONAL*
> *SCHOOLMASTER OF THIS TOWN.*
> *JOHN DIED MARCH 1852 AGED 8 yrs*
> *THOMAS DIED FEB 1856 AGED 6 yrs.*

John.

I was six when my brother came screaming into our world.
I'm an old man now, beyond age, and still a boy,
my name chipped neatly in the Cotswold stone,
as neat as my father's headline on a slate.
Soft stone, softer than death, too soft for time.
Five hundred seasons, sixty more, and the stone is brittle as a
    young boy's bone.
One frost, one storm, our names are gone.
You will have to leaf through copper-plated registers
to stumble on us by accident.
Children no longer slink on black streets, afraid of Thomas and me
We are too well dead for that, past haunting and remembering.
The evenings I like most are these,
when the town has gone about its business, gone away from us,
and I can sit on a flat stone beneath a yew, a red rose bush at the
    church door.
I conjure how it might have been.
Margaret Jones from the west side stands in the tower's shadow.
She was in my class and died herself at twenty-three, her two
    new-born already buried here.
Which sentence was the lighter?

Our going frightened her, woke her from restless sleep but little
did she think …

Mrs. Munn.
Schoolyard, churchyard, my husband knew them both.
Our children played in the one but never as noisily as the rest.
'Because of me,' he'd say. 'Because of what I am.'
Not so. I knew.
Their quietness was a listening for the whispers of death, so
      easily missed.
They listened.
First the pair of them and then just Thomas, listening even
      harder on his own.
The schoolyard gates flew open, without a push it seemed,
and the children escaped, in lines at first
but peeling off with careless grace into the rain,
the frost, the fog, the heat, into the world.
The churchyard gates opened another way
and the children stayed in lines,
cold in their timber frames like flowers struck by frost,
at a time of year when spring should be here but isn't.
In the school, my husband walks the corridor, closes the great
      door and turns his key.
The yard is too silent, all the children gone.
Not one to follow him down Broad Street, Castle Street,
no one to gallop in our gateway, just ahead of him.

Thomas.
I was two when my brother slipped, still, from our world,
the second month of spring, the last month of winter.
They took him down to St. Mary's and buried him inside the
      gate

in the rock hard clay, in the cold dead earth,
in the unrepentant ground, in the yard that never laughs.
What did I know of my brother?
I have no remembrance of him at all.
I knew, towards my own death, that he was dead.
When we came to pray on Sundays, he was lying there, beside
    the path.
I like October weather – no leaves fall here, all yews and grass.
But leaves blow in from the riverbank and I have some notion
    then
of what it is I have forgotten or never knew.
I should like to have heard the sea.
The thought of it consumed my childhood.
Perhaps it frightened me.

TOM MATHEWS

Lives

My father's cheek is rough.
I stand on wooden bricks to kiss him.
He is thirty-seven. I am six.

My mother's cheek is cheesecloth,
Soft as brie.
I stoop to kiss her.
I am fifty-six. She's eighty-three.

How old am I, my darling? Always eighteen,
Remembering our kisses in between.

Visiting the Locked Ward

Lights waltz like petals in her waterjug,
Watching which random choreography
She says, 'They talk about me. Later on
The birds will corkscrew out of the night like that.'

Penguin Beckett, packet of sanitary towels
Caught in the pulsing violet ambulance light.
'Love,' she says, 'is a mouse in a forest of owls
And I burn in the morning before I am delivered.'

And I burn in the morning.

JOAN McBREEN

The Story in the Shadows

I

I sit by the window. Outside, a willow.

Were my early songs out of tune,
my voice unheard?

People and things crowded in,
I allowed it, mistook all for the light.

Was I wrong? Should I have embraced
silence, learned to speak the truth?

I scattered memories to an unknown
world, to darkness and rain.

II

On this first day of spring, my pen
creaks across the page. I could write

of the crow on the oak branch
with his knowledge of the tree.

Instead I push the lamp aside, stare
straight ahead. Years have passed

faster than matchlight.

III

I kick a dead fish
along a beach, lift it with my foot.

It falls on wet sand, makes no sound.
Ebb tide in the west.

I sit on a rock, watch you walk away.

COLUM McCANN

As If There Were Trees

I WAS COMING HOME from my shift at the lounge when I saw Jamie in the field. The sun was going down and there were shadows on the ground from the flats. Jamie had his baby with him. She was about three months old. She was only in her nappy and she had a soother in her mouth. They were sitting together on a horse, not Jamie's horse – he'd sold his a long time ago to one of the other youngsters in the flats. This one was a piebald and it was bending down to eat the last of the grass in the goalmouth. Jamie was shirtless and his body was all thin. You could see the ribs in his stomach and you could see the ribs in the horse and you could see the ribs in the baby too. The horse nudged in the grass and it looked like all three of them were trying to get fed. There's nothing worse than seeing a baby hungry. She was tucked in against Jamie's stomach and he was just staring away into the distance.

The sun was going down and everywhere was getting red. There was red on the towers and there was red on the clinic and there was red on the windows of the cars that were burned out and there was red on the overpass at the end of the field. Jamie was staring at the overpass. It was only half-built, so the ramp went out and finished in mid-air. You could have stepped off it and fell forty feet.

Jamie used to work on the overpass until he got fired. They caught him with smack in his pocket when he was on the job. He complained to the Residents Committee because he was the only one from the flats on the overpass but there was no go. They couldn't help him because of the junk. They wanted to but couldn't. That was two weeks ago. Jamie had been moping around ever since.

Jamie started nudging his heels into the side of the horse. He was wearing his big black construction boots. You could see the heels making a dent in the side of the horse. I thought poor fucking thing, imagine getting kicked like that.

I was standing by the lifts and every time the doors opened there was a smell of glue and paint and shite came out and hit me. I was thinking about going home to my young ones who were there with my husband Tommy – Tommy looks after them since Cadbury's had the lay-offs – but something kept me at the door of the lift watching. Jamie dug his heels deeper into the horse and even then she didn't move. She shook her head and neighed and stayed put. Jamie's teeth were clenched and his face was tight and his eyes were bright as if they were the only things growing in him.

I've seen lots of men like that in The Well. The only thing alive in them is the eyes. Sometimes not even that.

Jamie was kicking no end and his baby was held tight to him now and the horse gave a little bit and turned her body in the direction of the overpass. Jamie stopped kicking. He sat and he watched and he was nodding away at his own nodding shadow for a long time, just looking at the men who were working late.

Four of them altogether. Three of them were standing on the ramp smoking cigarettes and one was on a rope beneath the ramp. The one below was swinging around on the rope. He looked like he was checking the bolts on the underside of the ramp. He had a great movement to him, I mean he would have made a great sort of jungle man or something, swinging through the trees, except of course there's no trees around here, you'd sooner get a brick of gold than a tree.

The ropeman was just swinging through the air and pushing his feet off the columns and his shadow went all over the place. It was nice to look at really. He was skinny and dark and I thought I recognised him from The Well, but I couldn't see his face I was so far away.

A lot of the men from the overpass come into The Well for lunchtime and even at night for a few jars. Most of them are Dubs although there's a few culchies and even a couple of foreigners. We don't serve the foreigners or at least we don't serve them quickly because there's always trouble. As Tommy says, The Well has enough trouble without serving foreigners. Imagine having foreigners, says Tommy. There's problems enough with the locals.

Not that Jamie was ever trouble. Jamie, when he came to The Well, he sat in the corner and sometimes even read a book, he was that quiet. He drank a lot of water sometimes, I think I know why but I don't make judgements. We were surprised when we heard about him shooting up on the building site though. Jamie never seemed like the sort, you know. Jamie was a good young fella. He was seventeen.

I looked back at the field and all of a sudden the sun went behind the towers and the shadows got all long and the whole field went much darker.

Jamie was still watching the ropeman on the overpass. The horse didn't seem to mind moving now. Jamie only tapped it with the inside of his heel and the horse got to going straight off. She went right through the goalposts and past all the burnt-out cars and she stepped around a couple of tyres and even gave a little kick at a collie that was snapping at her legs and then she went along the back of the clinic at the far end of the field. Jamie looked confident riding it bareback. Even though it was going very slow Jamie was holding on tight to his little girl so she wouldn't get bumped around.

In the distance the ropeman was still swinging under the overpass.

It was going through my head who the hell he was I couldn't remember. People were getting on and off the lift behind me and a couple of them stood beside me and asked, Mary what're you looking at? I just told them I was watching the overpass go up and they said fair enough and climbed into the lift. They must have thought I was gone in the head a bit, but I wasn't. I hadn't had a drink all day even after my shift.

I was thinking, jesus, Jamie what're you up to?

He was going in rhythm with the horse, slow, towards the overpass, the baby still clutched to him only in her nappy and maybe the soother still in her mouth I couldn't see. There were a couple of youngsters playing football not too far from the overpass and Jamie brought the horse straight through the middle of their jumpers which were on the ground for goalposts. One of the jumpers caught on the hoof of the horse and the goal was made bigger and the youngsters gave Jamie two fingers but he ignored them.

That was where the shadows ended. There was only a little bit of sun left but Jamie was in it now, the sun on his back and the sun on his horse and – like it was a joke – a big soft shite coming from the horse as she walked.

Jamie went up to the chickenwire fence that was all around the overpass to stop vandals but the chickenwire was cut in a million places and Jamie put one hand on the horse's neck and guided her through the hole in the wire.

He was gentle enough with the horse. He bent down to her back, and his baby was curled up into his stomach and all three of them could have been one animal.

They got through without a scrape.

That was when I saw the knife. It came out of his back pocket, one of those fold-up ones that have a button on them. The only reason I saw it was because he kept it behind his back and when he flicked the button it caught a tiny bit of light from the sun and glinted for a second. I said Fuck and began running out from the lifts through the car-park into the field towards the overpass. Twenty smokes a day but I ran like I was fifteen years old. I could feel the burning in my chest and my throat all dry and the youngsters on the football field stopping to look at me and saying jaysus she must have missed the bus. But I could see my own youngsters in Jamie, that's why I ran. I could see my young Michael and Tibby and even Orla, I could see them in Jamie. I ran I swear I'll never run like that again even though I was way too late.

I was only at the back of the clinic when Jamie stepped the horse right beneath the ramp. I tried to give a shout but I couldn't, there was nothing in my lungs. My chest was on fire, it felt like someone stuck a hot poker down my throat. I had to lean against the wall of the clinic. I could see everything very clearly now. Jamie had ridden the horse right underneath where the ropeman was swinging. Jamie said something to him and the ropeman nodded his head and shifted in the air a little on the rope. The ropeman looked up to his friends who were on the ramp. They gave him a little slack on the rope. The ropeman was so good in the air that he was able to reach into his pocket and pull out a packet of cigarettes as he swung. He flipped the lid on the box and negotiated the rope so he was in the air like an angel above Jamie's head.

Jamie stretched out his hand for the cigarette, took it, put it in his mouth and then said something to the ropeman, maybe thanks. The ropeman was just about to move away when the knife came and caught him on the elbow. I could see his face. It was pure surprise. He stared at his arm for the second it took the blood to leap out. Then he curled his body and he kicked at Jamie but Jamie's knife caught him on the leg. Jamie's baby was screaming now and the horse was scared and a shout came from the men up on the ramp. That's when I knew who they were. They were the Romanians, shouting in their own language. I remembered them from The Well the day we refused them service. Tommy said they were lucky to walk, let alone drink, taking our jobs like that, fucking Romanians. They didn't say a word that day, just thanked me and walked out of The Well. But jesus they were screaming now and their friend was in mid-air with blood streaming from him, it was like the strangest streak of paint in the air, it was paint going upwards because his friends were dragging on the rope, bringing him up to the sky, he wasn't dead of course, but he was just going upwards.

I looked away from the Romanians and at Jamie. He was calm as could be. He turned the horse around and slowly began to move away. He still had the baby in his arms and the cigarette in his mouth but he had dropped the knife and there were tears streaming from Jamie's eyes.

I leaned against the wall of the clinic and then I looked back towards the flats. There were people out in the corridors now and they were hanging over the balconies watching. They were silent. Tommy was there too with our young ones. I looked at Tommy and there was something like a smile on his face and I could tell he was there with Jamie and, in his loneliness, Tommy was crushing the Romanian's balls and he was kicking the Romanian's head in and he was rifling the Romanian's pockets and he was sending him home to his dark children with his ribs all shattered and his teeth all broken and I thought to myself that maybe I would like to see it too and that made me shiver, that made the night very cold, that made me want to hug Jamie's baby the way Jamie was hugging her too.

MOLLY McCLOSKEY

An excerpt from
Circles Around the Sun: In Search of a Lost Brother

THAT SPRING, MIKE PACKS his things and hits the road. For a while, nobody thinks much of it, assuming it is just more of the restlessness and lack of industry that he will soon grow out of. But after a couple weeks we stop hearing from him. Then we get a call from Danny, Mike's old high-school coach in Winston-Salem. Mike phoned Danny to say that he was travelling the country. 'Like Kerouac,' he told him – he knew Danny had a soft spot for Kerouac. He asked if he could come and stay. Mike used to visit Danny whenever he was home from Duke, and Sharon and the kids loved him, so Danny said, 'Yes, of course, come.'

The first few days Danny and Sharon didn't notice anything odd, except that Mike wasn't bathing. He played with the kids, went to the store with Sharon, entertained them all with tales of his travels across America – the crazy characters who picked him up hitching, the bear that almost ate him in Yellowstone. But after a week or so, he started acting strange – going to the nearby park at night, coming back wired, jittery, talking about 'Arabs' and sex, stories Danny and Sharon didn't know whether or not to believe. One night he told them a particularly weird tale, about going home with one of those 'Arabs'. When Danny asked him if he thought that was a good idea, Mike just looked at him and said matter-of-factly, 'It was neither a good nor a bad idea.' Mike was never aggressive with anyone, but his inhibitions in certain areas – mainly sexual – had simply vanished. Otherwise, he was perfectly coherent. This was what Danny and Sharon found so strange, the bizarre behaviour side by side with lucidity. Not knowing what to do, they phoned my parents, who sent money for Mike to return to Oregon.

The local high school is close enough that Robin, just turned eighteen and in her final year, can walk there from our house. One day, soon after that phone call from Danny and Sharon, she is coming into the driveway after school when our father comes out the front door to meet her. She can see that he is extremely shaken, not quite in possession of himself. He gives her a hug and tells her he loves her very much – not his usual greeting when she arrives home from school – then leads her inside to where her eldest brother is stretched out on a bed.

The last time Robin saw Mike, he was just an ordinary hippy, heading off on his Kerouacian rambles. Clearly, something has changed. He is skinnier than he has ever been, and yet he does not look physically ill. Whatever is wrong with him is more complicated than that. He stares at the ceiling, like she isn't even there. She doesn't think she's ever seen anyone like this up close, certainly not anyone she knows. It scares her. She has no idea what to do, and nobody has explained anything to her. At some point, when her parents are out of the room, she sits on the twin bed opposite and attempts to make conversation with him. Small talk with Mike has never been easy for her – she finds him aloof and somewhat intimidating – but she tries, asking him where he's been on his travels. Even as she says it, she can hear how silly the question sounds.

He stares at the ceiling while his sister fidgets. Finally, he says, 'Robin, your words are meaningless to me.'

It's a Friday. My parents don't want to take Mike to a psychiatric hospital, but they do want him to see a doctor. The only one they can get hold of that weekend is an acquaintance of theirs, a young psychiatrist who has long hair and wears love beads. When they bring Mike to his office the following day, the psychiatrist talks to them, then to Mike alone, then to all of them together. He asks Mike some questions.

'If you saw a letter on the ground with an address and a stamp on it, what would you do?'

'I'd put it on the window-sill so it wouldn't blow away,' Mike says.

'If you were standing with a group of people at a bus stop, what would they be talking about?'

'Me,' Mike says.

There is no test that provides a definitive diagnosis of schizophrenia. Diagnosis is made on the basis of an interview with a clinician, who assesses the presence or absence of certain symptoms and the period of time over which they have persisted. Aside from the psychotic symptoms – hallucinations (typically auditory) and delusions (fixed, false beliefs) – there are also the so-called negative symptoms (a diminishment in normal thoughts and speech and an absence of normal emotional expression) and the disorganized symptoms, which include confused thoughts, memory problems, and difficulty concentrating, following instructions and completing tasks. The long-haired psychiatrist diagnoses schizophrenia that day.

Despite the doctor's explanation, my parents have no idea what it means, really, this ugly word, the word that from this day forth will define and describe and circumscribe their son. There is a terrible unceremoniousness about it, this upending of their reality, the way they are expected to just absorb the news.

Late that night, my mother sits on the built-in bench in the kitchen, the big plate-glass window behind her and the blackness beyond, her stomach churning as she asks herself again and again, *What is happening?* Apparently, Mike has done some drugs, serious ones, the ones that make you think you're Jesus or that you can fly. Are they what's done this to him? Or was it something she and Jack did, something *she* did? The concept of the schizophrenogenic mother has not yet been entirely discredited. She doesn't exactly fit the bill (overprotective, dominant but rejecting), but it will be many years before she is free of the fear that some action, or else a more consistent feature of her mothering, was the cause of his illness.

Mike, not surprisingly, does not accept the verdict. He keeps insisting his parents are the ones who need help. The weekend isn't easy. While my mother makes dinner, Mike walks around the kitchen barking like a dog.

⌢

Soon stabilized by the antipsychotics, Mike spends his time playing the harmonica, meditating and reading books by Maharishi Mahesh Yogi. I turn them over and look at Maharishi's photo on the back, his fleshiness and glinting eyes and luxuriant grey beard suggestive of a sensuality I find creepy. Mike has a bushy beard, too, and heavy black horn-rimmed glasses. He sleeps on a big blue waterbed, and sometimes we sit on the bed together in the lotus position and he tries to teach me the harmonica.

I am nine. I do not know what to think about either him or his trouble. It is, after all, adult trouble, and if the words *paranoid schizophrenia* have filtered down to me at all (or have been communicated in some solemn family conference), they have not been accompanied by any in-depth explanation; we are living in an age in which adults have not yet begun to burden children with well-intentioned attempts to put life's dreadful phenomena into age-appropriate language. My thoughts and feelings about Mike are shaped by a mix of intuition, overheard or handed-down bits of information and misinformation, guesswork, fear, fascination and the instinctive bond of siblings. In my world of unknowing, half of me adores him and the other half feels vaguely repelled.

By June, he is well enough to get work as a freelance gardener, work he will continue through that summer. He begins a vegetable garden of his own in our backyard. He toys with the idea of getting his teaching certificate, though at the moment there are more teachers than jobs. But while his future remains uncertain (*His plans for the fall are still indefinite,* my mother writes, *but he is happy, tan, healthy – no booze, ciggies or pot . . .*), everyone, including him, still assumes he has one, that the madness of late spring was a drug-induced breakdown from which he will emerge.

Dear Fanny and Nony,

Greetings from the rain capital of the world, Portland, Oregon. Today I was out trying to make a few bucks for summer travel so it decided to hail for ten minutes and then rain the rest of the morning. I just hope it doesn't frost and kill the garden I'm growing. We've got asparagus, lettuce and spinach coming up with some tomato plants. Mom and Dad came home last night they're all tan and relaxed. They brought me a Mickey Mouse T-shirt for my birthday. Nothing compared to what you gave me thank you thank you thank you thank you. It's been so long I don't know what else to say except that I'll put the money to good use this summer. Dad's talking about renting a house boat and sailing up to Canada from Washington. I'm more for back packing and beaching in California myself. We'll compromise somehow. Not much else to say except I think about you both a lot. John and I may be coming east this summer. We'll see you somehow.

Love,

Mike

The letter, written less than two months after his first serious trouble, shows no signs of psychological disturbance. Though clearly eager to be on the road again, he sounds very much a part of the family. Recently, we have added to our brood: a dog, whom Mike picked out from the pound and to whom he will remain lovingly devoted for the twelve years of her life, often preferring her company to that of humans. For reasons unknown, he christens her Munka. She is a mongrel, not proud or intelligent or beautiful, but excessively affectionate. Unable to contain her joy when one of us arrives home, she waggles her whole bottom and pisses with excitement, the voluminousness of the stream in direct proportion to the intensity of her affection, its force and duration greater if you've been out of town.

Mike grows lean and fit working on his gardens. Sometimes he takes me along when he goes to one particular client – a sweet elderly widow who lives in a mock-Tudor house on the lake shore. She feeds me petite sandwiches at an ornate wrought-iron table overlooking the water, and while Mike works I swim in the lake and loll on the dock, pretending that this is where we live. He and I have a way of being alone when together that seems to suit us both. From his point of view, our affinity may be based on the fact that I am the only one in the house young enough to be ignorant of what his recent diagnosis means.

He has given me two souvenirs from his recent travels. One is a small rust-coloured coral square that has been etched by natural forces with what looks like cuneiform, so that it might be an ancient tablet in miniature. The other is a segment of pocked coral, its surface inlaid with dozens of tiny fossilized sea urchins. No one in my family has ever deemed anything so small, so unimproved upon, worthy of cherishing. Taking my cue from Mike, I regard both of these objects as exotic treasures and display them on the shelf in my bedroom.

≈)

Our moment of affinity turns out to be brief. By the following year I am old enough to be embarrassed by his oddness, to want to distance myself from whatever is wrong with him. At the same time, I fail to take it seriously. Some days after school, my best friend and I skulk around, spying on him through windows, excited less by his fairly ordinary activities than by our secret vantage point, and a feeling of superiority we don't begin to understand. He is like a caged creature brought back from some exotic isle, the only adult in our midst who might actually do something not just odd but totally bizarre, noteworthy enough to be entered in the little logbook in which we keep a record of all the silly doings of our lives. Sometimes we ring the front bell, then dash into the rhododendron bushes and watch as he comes to the door, first puzzled, then spooked, then annoyed.

We are trying, in the colloquial sense, to drive him crazy. It is nothing personal; we like to play this irritating game with lots of people, just as we like to hide things people need and rifle through our parents' personal belongings and call strangers picked at random from the phone book. Or, if it *is* personal, it is only so in the sense that we, being children, naturally visit our tortures upon those in whom we detect vulnerability. I know that there is something strange about Mike, but I have no idea that his problems are related to a periodic inability to distinguish between what is real and what is not. And so we ring the bell and run away. We knock on the windowpanes, then press ourselves, out of sight, against the outer wall.

My failure to grasp the gravity of his condition might be partly accounted for by the gap in our ages. Because there are enough years between us that I can't remember him being any other way, he seems to me more an eccentric uncle who's come to stay than a once-brilliant brother unravelling before me. And I still assume – so unconsciously it doesn't register as an assumption – that nothing truly calamitous can ever befall our family.

(Penguin Ireland, 2011)

MIKE McCORMACK

Solar Bones
from a work in progress

… and I think it must have been this same sort of confusion which consumed my father and unravelled his mind in that last year of his life when he lost his grip on the world completely and withdrew to the old house where there was only himself and the dog to keep each other company in those fateful days after Onnie's death when the full weight of her absence must have come upon him with so much fear and loneliness that it eclipsed his grief entirely in disbelief at the fact that his wife of over forty years could ever leave him for any reason whatsoever – death included – leave him behind and all alone now, a fate he had never envisioned nor prepared himself for so that when it did come it scrambled his sense of the world so thoroughly it was as if something essential to the proper order and balance of the universe had been casually set aside and replaced with some new circumstance which so keenly insulted something delicate within him that

in no time at all his strength and resolve came undone, he slackened and lost interest in the world before withdrawing completely to the house with the dog where, in the half light of those narrow rooms, behind drawn curtains, his confusion and grief deepened to that fatal awkwardness with which there is no reasoning so that very suddenly he grew angry and rancorous and fell out with myself and Eithne, took against us with such decisive vehemence in the week after Onnie's funeral that we did not have time to fathom the proper cause or reason for it but were nevertheless left in no doubt by his rage that some shameful blame had accrued to both of us because he dismissed us from behind the closed front door, telling us to leave and not come back and calling us a

—a shower of cunts and nothing but

his curse upon us the day he sold off all his livestock and hens, leaving just himself and Rex alone in the house when he barred the two gates coming into the yard, secured them with two balks of timber tied from pillar to pillar so that the postman had to climb up over the sod fence and walk down the path to shove the letters and mass cards under the door because that too was bolted and

all this happened before Onnie's month's mind mass had been said but by which time he had begun to show the first signs of letting himself go by growing a beard which threatened to engulf his whole head – a genuinely shocking sight on a man who had been clean shaven the whole of his seventy odd years but which now he would not hear a word against except to say that his father had had one and his father before him had had one also and our Lord – who was a better man than either of them – had had one also and if a beard was good enough for those men then it was good enough for him also and that was an end to it but

this marked the point at which he really began to neglect himself, no wash or shave and the same clothes on him day in day out while he grew thinner and thinner inside them with the shirt hanging open over his narrow chest and his trousers barely hanging on his hips – but the hair and beard still growing – thickening like a wild furze around his head – but no fire or heat on in the house anymore so that it got damp and filthy and there was nothing but the smell of piss meeting me at the door those few times he let me in to see him with a few bits and pieces for him and he was sitting there in the dark, all alone in the glare of the television screen with a can of fly spray on the table and Bosco on the television and the dog out eating the grass along the margins of the road and it was around this time also, and for whatever reason, that

he upped and bought a new tractor

I swear to god

a span new David Browne which cost thousands and he began talking of his plans to hire it out to agricultural contractors for silage making and turf cutting and so on, with him driving of course – this man who by now could hardly walk without the aid of a stick, the power in his legs gone and him near crippled with the dampness in his bones – and he housed the tractor in the old shed beside the haggard and put a fine galvanise roof over it but that's as much as he ever did with it because if he started it five or six times after that then that was about the height of it because he never did any work with it whatsoever – who was going to hire a man who could hardly walk, tractor or no tractor – so it stayed there in the shed with the same fill of diesel it had arrived in the yard with and whenever he wasn't gazing at it from the kitchen window he was out with a cloth buffing and wiping it across the windscreen or polishing the headlamps, caring for it like it was his special toy, which of course it was and all this nothing but his own second childhood – and all this care and attention for a tractor when his own house was going to wrack and ruin around him with dampness running down the walls of every room and a scraw of black mould growing in the bathroom and

sometimes, if you were passing you might see him standing at the gable of the house, leaning on the stick and smoking, watching the cars going the road to town in the evening but, if you stopped to talk to him over the fence he'd take off like a frightened hen and you'd hear him pulling the bolts on the door from the road and you could imagine him sitting there alone in the waning light of the kitchen, watching the television, day in day out, wasting away in confusion and neglect while winter closed in around him and the television stayed on but the bulbs started to go out in one room after another as doors were closed for the last time on these same rooms and as bottles and newspapers piled up on the chairs and the dresser and the sofa under the window while all around him the house gradually came apart with paint peeling and curtains fraying and doors swelled from the dampness till that night came when he was sleeping in the room at the far end and he woke up in the early hours to a horrible creaking and smashing as the apex

of the gable fell out at the end of his bed and there he was sitting
up looking out on the hills and the stars in the night sky, watching
Rex barking and running off in fright into the moonlight so that
   two days later
   I stood outside the barred gate pleading with him to sign a
grant application form so that he could get the house renovated,
the whole thing sealed and insulated, windows and doors and a
new roof, all he had to do was put his name at the bottom of the
application form, that's all he had to do, I would look after the
rest, organise the paperwork and contract the job out to a registered
builder, all he had to do was sign his name, but would he sign
   would he fuck sign
   —I will in my fuck sign
   he said, from inside the gate,
   —I'll sign fuck all or put an X on anything either
   he roared
   —coming here with your fucking forms looking for signatures
– by Jesus, you must think I'm very innocent if you expect me to
fall for that one – but I'll tell you one thing now and not two things
– I know well what your game is boyo – I'll sign that form and the
next thing I'll find myself in the county home and this house will
be sold out from under me and yourself and your sister dividing it
up between ye, isn't that what you're up to, isn't that what you're
after
   —it's not what I'm up to and it's not what I'm after
   —like fuck its not – I'm telling you now and for the last time,
take your application form and your grant and your contracts and
fuck off back to where you came from and
   and that's the thanks I got
   standing outside the gate waving the form at him, begging
him to see reason and telling him that I was for his good and that
this was the right thing to do and all I wanted was that he'd have
a roof over his head and warmth – a small bit of comfort living
on his own and my hand to god, I had no intention of putting

him in the county home or any other home for that matter because this was his home, I knew that, no one wanted to put him away and

my heart was twisted in my chest with a desperate love for this man who had been the hero of my life but who now was so confused he was apparently incapable of seeing who or what was good for him and this above all was what cut me to the bone – how this man who had moved so confidently through the world, this man whom I had seen dismantle universes and navigate by pure instinct – this man, could now misread the world so completely that he could see no good in anything anymore, not even in his own son who stood outside the gate with my temper gone and my patience gone but still pleading with him and pleading for myself that he should

—sign the fucking form, for the love of Jesus

but I was talking to his back now because he was hobbling away down the path to the house and I watched him go inside and pull the door behind him and even at that distance I could hear the bolts ramming home and I stood there a few minutes longer, hardly able to move from heartbreak and despair before I eventually pushed myself off the gate and drove back home to phone my sister that evening and tell her what had happened and so begin a long argument with her, trying to convince her that I had done all I could do to help him, begged and pleaded with him, pushed the forms under his nose but it was no good, nothing was any good, there was no talking to him, and what the hell did she want me to do, what more could I do, wrestle him to the ground and force him to sign them, was that what she wanted because if she thought she could do a better job she was welcome to try because I was at my wits end with the whole fucking thing … and I put the phone down with a bang or she put the phone down with a bang, I don't know, and I opened a bottle of Jameson to sit drinking in this kitchen till the early hours of the morning and that was the last word I spoke to Eithne until

six months later when he was found lying on the concrete walk
outside the house by a neighbour over the village, Mattie Moran,
who was on his way into town to collect his dole when he spotted
him from the road as he was passing and pulled up to hop in over
the wall and go down on his knee beside him, to lay his ear on his
chest and check if he was breathing before picking him up and
laying him into the back of the car, stick and all, Mattie telling me
afterwards that

    —it was like lifting a bundle of sticks – there was more meat
on a sparrow's ankle and he

    drove him to the hospital where he stayed for the next three
weeks and was washed and fed while they ran all those tests on him
which finally diagnosed the pancreatic cancer which killed him
within a couple of weeks, by which time there was less than six
stone of him in the bed and only that he still had the wild head of
hair on him you could hardly see his face in the middle of the
pillow but I combed it and did my best to tidy it and then I put
him in his grandchild's confirmation suit because he was now so
shrunk none of his own would fit him and we lowered his coffin
into the grave beside Onnie on the 27th November and I stood
there with Mairead and Agnes and Darragh beside me, the four of
us huddled together in the chilly sunshine reciting a decade of the
rosary, the first glorious mystery the Resurrection, our murmured
prayers carried away on the breeze and while I stood there I would
not have thought it a moment for the big questions – life, the
universe and the whole dam thing – I did find myself sifting
through the tragedy of his last year and wondering to myself whose
idea of justice was satisfied in this mans final confusion and
humiliation and wondering also to what end or purpose had he
been allowed to waste away to such ragged ignominy but as I say
it may not have been a fit time or the place for such questions but
then again is there ever a time or place …

HUGH McFADDEN

Far Behind the Snow

The strange poignancy of snow in the city:
of awakening to blinds on my window
framed and bordered by startling light;
of the white marshmallow softness to the eye
of undisturbed snow cushioning my garden;
three new daffodils, their fragile yellow crowns
forlorn against the pure white under the bare
cherry-blossom tree still dreaming of April.

Why should unaccustomed precipitation
in February arouse sad emotion?
Is it that snow recalls Errigal for me,
its peak a white cone in winter –
or Muckish with brilliant mantle,
or Sliabh Sneachta, so aptly-named?

Snow's the real psychedelic experience:
watching floating flakes swirl and dance in the air.

Good Vibes

On my way to listen to
Paul Durcan read his verse at
The National Gallery,
who should I run into –
just down from the Shelbourne

on St. Stephen's Green – but
men in fluorescent jackets
bearing this great legend:

'National Vibration
Monitoring Service' –

shades of
'Danger: Men at Work'.

And if that doesn't shake your
tambourine, my friend, early
in the morning, then listen
to all those good vibrations.

IGGY McGOVERN

The Cure

We loved her tales of The Big House ghosts,
the coach-and-pair and headless driver
raking up the drive and the devil corked
in a bottle buried beneath the step,
(the Priest reluctantly brought in
where the Minister had failed)
and something about a great black dog,
prowling the village on moonless nights.
Almost too late we came to know
this beast was a frequent visitor,
biting her hand, breaking her heart;
and with the help of a few good friends
we buried it deep at the huntsman's cross
and it never found the road home.

MÁIGHRÉAD MEDBH

A Capacity for Wings

Before psychology ruled the world, She tripped on the borderline
and it turned to dust. she took several steps and looked back.
    Still She
stood on the first stop and sent orderly sounds from an echoing
    mouth.
she rubbed herself against the ground and smoothly slid up a
    shaft
the same naked colour as herself. At the tip she chewed and
    vegetised.

It was different grass, more chewable, and they couldn't see it.
    Large
concepts rolled from their mouths and shook her perch.
    Blowing, they
didn't see her tower sway and her head bruise from the drops of
    moisture.
They began a procession She trailed. There were trumpets and
    tambourines
and in a sudden morph, clanging white cranes and booming red
    cadillacs.

She wore mismatched weeds and stared at Her somnolent feet,
    knew
their song for a split logos but sang it all the same, while in
    cacaphon
the green slunch and slitherpop and slopslop led her headdown
    from
the tower to make patties of the clay. She tried these for beds,
    bellied
them and took their cool touch for fingers saying come.

Sweet it was when she and the clay yes combined. It was slow
   cooking.
she slept the way of the sane and let the ideal lover people her
   dreams.
He was long and thin and stood pragmatic in a modern interior.
   Then
he was Plantagenet in hose and cote-hardie, witticising like her
   personal
clown. Every man She ever knew. Hidden rivers flooded to the
   quickening

thrust of an unsuitable eye. Pleasure sans the merciless combat of
   light.
The march and everything withered but she in her tight wrap and
muted blood ran a dark operation that was nothing willed,
   therefore art.
Dawn dived in and an oligarchy of foreign colours threw her
   over to the
procession. she tried to walk but couldn't. Fly neither. Stalled.

Flapflap she did finally and made things change. Back to the
   tower again.
Lone, but it was hers at least, unlike the rhythmic riling throng.
But the wind overfluttered her, turned her small as a grain of
   rice. Wanting
to be served, she wished herself on a plate, closed eyes pursed
   lips. They
found Her underfoot and stepped back, did what they do,
   formed a circle.

The mad stampede they said had done it. she let them think so.
   But it had been
a white crane that lifted her, the only thing she saw that reached
   someway skyward.

she had moved out onto its teeth, wanting to see and wanting to
    be closed up,
high as butterfly-possible. When it tipped over she was its, that
    unity,
gashed her wings on it before letting every stray and ordered
    colour, each herSelf go.

Breathing

With thanks to Van Morrison

I'm breathing not living
spewed from the bed by habit
wonder am I already given to the high winds
such a space hums between me and what they call world.
I don't live as I love
or where brain could breathe
or where smiles rise to the surface more readily than shrieks.
Why do I walk this parching ground
pulse drumming the rhythm of an order I can't fathom
gasping from oasis to mirage
lost as the unexamining sky?
In a time of achievement I'm staring out the window
at a shivering tree
working in a two-bit job
putting on a face and the air of success
when I regret every minute of my unimportance
the years spent waiting for life to drop in
the moony pub nights
the drools and delusions I gave energy to.
I fight and get nowhere quick
no hour like the last
no-one reflecting because *where is your face?*

And these love acts between me and the mechanical substitute
because it's not my time.
Is it ever my time?
But time is manically tapping
knock-knocking
jiving at my expense
that unhuman groove sounding as I inch helpless towards the void.
The dog needs walking
another drag.
Stick the earphones in the iPod,
hope the battery at least is charged.
Here's the same old limited path
rabbits scurrying from the enemy scent
trees growing up and out who cares
the last green enclave for miles.
Nature in a nutshell.
           Press a button and a split second says
           with an upbeat drum
           that something is about to shift
           is about to cross
           to the *Bright Side of the Road.*
           Van Morrison can help my feet – I can't –
           or my lightened arms
           or my suddenly fuck-it-all body
           that says by itself
           let those others think what they want
           let them look nervously away
           because what is there to lose
           except this moment in the morning air
           dancing to the only accompaniment
           on the bright side of the dark matter
           on all sides sun because
           well because
I'm breathing

PAULA MEEHAN

Diamond Faceted, His Breath

'Which is heavier – a ton of coal or a ton of feathers?'

My father's death lay on me like a feather;
his own hard fought for last mortal breath
was diamond in the radiant Samhain weather.

Light as the pages that fell from *The Mirror* –
TOXIC DUMP: BANK BILLIONS LOST: TEST TUBE BIRTH:
– my father's breath could scarce disturb a feather.

The going was hard at Dundalk, at Uttoxeter;
Red Era a horse he believed had some worth,
given the right ground, the right kind of weather.

The half-done crossword: ten across, eight letters,
daughter. Nine down, bold – no! – wild. Seven down, hearth.
The words themselves as light as any feather

I could carry every step of my future
on the smooth or rocky contours of my path
whatever the news, whatever the breaking weather.

In the hospice garden, a child's laughter
falling like dry leaves to the hard black earth
was my father's death – the weight of a feather,
as I roved out into the coming winter weather.

LIA MILLS

Adapted extracts from **In Your Face**

In 2006, writer Lia Mills was diagnosed with advanced mouth cancer that required radical surgery to her face and neck, and the removal of bone from her leg to rebuild her face. After surgery she was given a course of radiotherapy. Throughout her illness, she kept records of what happened. An edited version of her notebooks was published as a book, In Your Face. *The following extracts were written during the interval between 5th April, when a biopsy was performed on her cheek, and 4th May, the date of surgery.*

1. AFTER THE BIOPSY

5 April

I emerge from the consulting room, shocked and sore. The waiting room has filled up, but I can't look at anyone directly. I don't feel like myself anymore. A piece of bloody gauze hangs from my mouth.

I text my sister, who meets me at the train and takes me for lunch, but I can't eat. We go to a pharmacy and each of us buys separate packets of painkillers. They're all for me, but the law allows only one packet per person. It reminds me of buying slimming tablets back in the seventies, when I used to pad myself up with sweaters and coats and do the rounds of various chemists, to avoid suspicion.

A ghastly little old woman skips in front of me to an empty seat in the DART and laughs into my face – she's beaten me to it. There are plenty of other seats, and usually I'd tell myself not to react, you never know what people have on their minds. Today I feel such rage I could throw her off the train. I nearly forget to get off myself, I'm staring so hard at the sunshine, the sea, schoolkids pulling off their jumpers in the heat, daffodils.

6 April

The pain in my cheek throbs and swells, like a musical note; it flowers, a dark bloom with thorns. It's a filter, a veil of colour.

I keep thinking about the man with the heavy overcoat and the black hat who used to walk along our street with his stiffening, slowing dog. They used to be there at the same time every morning as I drove the girls to school. A few months ago I started to notice that they came later and later in the day, the two of them moving more slowly. Step, pause. Step, pause. Who was keeping whom on track? My breath used to catch, every time, because I wondered if this might be the last time I'd see them. We used to say hello. He'd raise his hat and smile, a very old smile. We talked about the weather. I haven't seen them now for weeks even though the days are lightening.

7 April

I venture out to Penney's, where I get overwhelmed by the summer profusions, by the ludicrousness of my situation: shopping for things I'll need if I have to go into hospital when everyone else has arms full of bikinis and towels, flipflops dangling from their fingers. Meanwhile the weight in my cheek grows, the heat of the lump and its throb make me feel conspicuous. For some reason, it makes me think of a kidney, hot and toxic. It pulls me down, a tug at the root. It goes up the cheekbone and deep into the jaw now as well, radiates, an acrid little blade, tongue of flame. Blisters of fizz on the tongue. That little pouch of saliva, silky and heavy.

Still, I head off for Tesco and do the shopping – the place is bedlam. I watch everyone. Whatever fears, worries or wild ambition we harbour, we go through the same motions, the numb dance of fill and empty, of cards and cash, the rituals of greeting and farewell.

8 April

A rotten night. I've been on the internet again and now I'm sleepless with pain and sudden anxieties, projecting all the possibilities.

These days I sneak long looks at my daughters and grandson when they aren't paying attention, ring my husband for no reason. He's working in London. I have an appalled recognition of the work I still want to do, the sheer extent of it, and how far I am from getting there – I'm not even in the room yet! Still gathering notes. Yesterday, on the radio, Seamus Heaney read a poem for John McGahern. Introducing it, he talked about the sadness of loss, but the sense of a work completed. No one could say that for me, not even close.

I don't know how to deal with talking to people, who to tell and why – I don't know what to say. I don't want to moan and bleat for no reason. It's easier to say nothing. So, when a friend, preoccupied with her own, very real, disasters, cancels an arranged meeting and says, I'll be in touch, I think, well, maybe you won't – but she doesn't know what's on my mind, how could she; her attention is bent elsewhere. How many times have I been the unknowing person in that equation?

When I do tell people – it's interesting to see who's determined to avoid the pit that's opening at my feet, who doesn't notice it at all, and who takes it in. The thing is, we are all really alone. There are those who stretch out their hands to you (and mean it) while others fold their hands into their pockets, around what's theirs, and look away.

Now, when I talk about having time to write, I don't mean a week in Annaghmakerrig. A good twenty-five years might do it.

2. AFTER DIAGNOSIS

Cancer. The crab. I know it's inaccurate to link the star sign with the disease, but it describes the way I imagine my tumour perfectly: hard-shelled and ugly, flesh-coloured, swelling and sucking at my cheek.

13 April

It's Beckett's birthday. He suffered from a painful cyst in his mouth that required surgery when he was older than I am now. This cheers me a little, because he lived so far and so productively beyond it. That great photo is pinned to my noticeboard at home. He's staring at my empty chair.

In the X-ray department I'm given a plastic folder to carry to Nuclear Medicine. The label on it reads:

Lia Mills. Squamous cell carcinoma right cheek, for pre-op staging.

I'm shocked when I read it. It's too blunt. The plastic folder contains the dense, revealing negatives of X-rays; inner worlds, arcane shapes and smoky shadows. You could mount these on an exhibition wall, give dimensions, name the medium. But this is not art. I feel the weight of my diagnosis now.

The tide of shock recedes and I take my place in the waiting room. I wonder if this is how the knowledge of a diagnosis like mine works, that it comes over you, then retreats while you get your bearings, then returns. An incoming tide doesn't flood in all at once with the force of a burst dam. It sends warning, each successive wave advancing a little farther than the last until the tidal lands are flooded. Then the retreat begins. My tide of understanding is on the way in, but it's not fully here yet. High tide comes later.

15 April

There is something about this tumour being externally visible. People look for the swelling on my cheek, then their eyes jump away. Has my voice already changed? Is this a one-way journey? Even if it is, there's nothing to be done but to keep going. We laugh and play cards, offer each other chocolate.

16 April (Easter Sunday)

I'm allowed home for the day. On the way out we take detours around the route of the parade commemorating the Easter Rising. I'm struck again by the crooked charm of the quays and how I love the many sweetnesses of this city. We pass children feeding swans on the canal; low tide at Scotsman's Bay, boats grounded in sludge at Bulloch. The sea throws up diamonds of light in Killiney Bay.

It's bliss to be home, with people dropping in, bringing the flowers I'm not allowed to keep in hospital: they've been banned, supposedly to reduce the spread of infection. My sisters are here. Messages tumble into my phone. Kindness and offers of help.

Everyone is eager to tell me stories of survival. What I want to know is, if everyone in the stories survives, who dies?

Time pours away so fast, at home. Every time I look up, another hour has passed.

17 April

It feels as if I'm on a train that's been shunted off onto a parallel track and now I'm in a siding. Everyday life thunders past on the main line. I can do nothing but wait for the signals to shift before I resume my journey. People ask if I'm angry, but I'm not. Not yet, anyway. Some trouble waits for all of us and this is mine right now. I keep thinking about Anne LaMott's idea, that we're all in it, up to our necks, but what matters is the kind of people we choose to be in the face of that.

Yeats believed that the key to a character is to discover which myth they embody. My myth keeps changing. Enter Ariadne with her simple gift … but that story ends badly for everyone. What if she'd kept her thread for herself, found her way out of her own myth, back to everyday life? Sounds good to me.

18 April

Cancer of the mouth – other people have the same reaction as I did. They didn't know it was something you could get. I should have known. You can get cancer anywhere.

The crab is awake, sucking and squeezing. Sharp anchors scrape against my jaw all night. In the morning it's like a boiled sweet lodged in my cheek, as if I could suck on it.

My mouth is eating me.

I'm fasting again. I have to go for a PET^2 scan to determine if the cancer has spread and if so, how far.

The nurse who explains the procedure tells me that she has a degenerative disease herself. Months ago she was barely able to lift her arm. Now she looks fit and healthy.

'I'm living proof,' she says. 'Don't give up.'

These scans remind me of old spy films: searchlights and waste ground. Shadows moving into position. The radioactive glucose is carried in a heavy metal box, handled with gloves. The isotope slithers, cold, up my arm. After the injection they dim the lights. I have to lie still for an hour before entering the scanner: no jigging about, no talking. Reading, I'm told, can give false results because during the scan glucose is drawn to places where there is activity in the body, and reading draws it to the eyes.

I'm so intrigued by this idea that it keeps me busy for the hour. I wonder what effect thinking might have. What my imagination looks like.

The doctor comes in. She offers me a cool, boneless hand. She asks about the lump in a way that no one else has done. Does it hurt? Can she touch it? I guide her hand. She asks to see it. I show her. She says thanks, she doesn't often get the chance to look at a tumour directly. I don't suppose many people do.

They strap me to a thin table and feed me into a noisy plastic tunnel with a keen red eye of its own. It revs and clicks while the motor spins, but I am coccooned. Untouchable. People say the scanner is claustrophobic but it doesn't bother me. I close my eyes.

Celia's poem, where a CT scan 'snaps poems I have written, poems // I have yet to write,'[3] keeps me and my involuted imagination company.

3. AFTER THE FIRST OPERATION, TO INSERT A FEEDING TUBE

22 April
Each shock is new. This post-op state – of sudden weakness, pain, vulnerability, need – is a stronger version of what I felt after the biopsy. If this is what I'm like now, what will I be like after the major operation? I'm like a raw recruit who gets wounded during training.

The crab is fizzing and spitting today, as with rage – that creepy feeling that it's still trying to do its lethal work, embedding itself wherever it can find purchase. The burn of my tongue against it. What will it be like to have half a face?

23 April
It's Census day and I won't be home at midnight, so I can't be included on the form. I won't be counted as one of the family, I'll be registered in the hospital instead. I hate the way that makes me feel.

I'm allowed out again. On the way home we go for a short walk at Sandycove and see a seal swimming towards the Forty Foot. The water in the bay is navy and sparkling. Inside the walls of Bulloch it turns green. The gorse on the hill is bright as fire. The girls have got me gorgeous flowers. Orange cannas, sunflowers and a tall one that looks like a yucca, yellow. Tied with orange straw. My very own flares.

We go for a drive. At Shanganagh, I think how we've never gone in to look at the cemetery, although we've meant to do it. We've bantered about whether or not the price of a grave has gone up, like every other inch of real estate around here. It would be impossible to joke about it today.

The gorse riots across Wicklow, the birds shrill out mad songs. How quickly we are changed. A month ago we were up here in the ice, got stuck in snow at the side of the road. Today, it's lambs and gorse, fast-running water and soft green mounds. That phrase 'what doesn't kill you makes you stronger' spools through my brain as I take in signs of early spring and summer. I plan on getting a whole lot stronger.

We drive past Luggala and stop to look down into the corrie. It sparkles black, ringed with browns and greys, a green with metal in it. Dark. On towards the Sally Gap. It's like being on a brown moon up here. Bare silver trees crouch in the folds and creases of hills. Glencree, winding down old roads through older trees and home again. It's ridiculous how much I love that silly road, the ramshackle, meaningless village where we live.

24 April
(At a family meeting with the surgical team, we're told the planned extent of surgery and follow-up treatment)

The prognosis, according to conventional statistics, is fairly bleak, but I'm a young woman, they say, without a trace of irony, and healthy up until now. There is a chance, as with all major surgery, that I won't survive the operation. Things can go wrong, but they wouldn't put me through the operation if they didn't think I had a fighting chance.

I ask what I can do to prepare myself.

You might want to think about your will, is the response.

The room goes very quiet.

Then they repeat that if they didn't think I had a chance, they wouldn't do this surgery, they wouldn't waste their time or mine.

They warn me against unmonitored and potentially inaccurate information on the internet. They suppose I'll go there anyway.

In fact I've decided to trust them, but I don't say so. I think I really didn't take it in before now.

I want to live.

How melodramatic and clichéd that sounds, but it's the truest thing I can think of, right here and now.

⤚

1. Anne Lamott, *Bird by Bird: Some Notes on Writing and Life* (Pantheon Books, 1994).
2. PET, Positron Emission Tomography.
3. Celia de Freine, 'In the Land of Wince and Whinny,' from *Scarecrows at Newtownards* (Scotus Press, 2005).

(from *In Your Face,* Penguin Ireland, 2007)

JUDITH MOK

Beethoven in New York

Fur Elise

This night is on me like a blank sheet.
I have to write
Of people playing music that
Fills the subway with my submerged sounds,
As if I am a whale vibrating through the thick of times,
Communicating that my name is: Beethoven,
A man of music in a storm of voices,
A choir, an army of American instruments,
People playing my music, people judging me,
How I rode this crushing wave of emotions.

I wake to chaos and constellations in my head,
Thinking: I will have to tell her
I heard this choir supporting some statement about me,
Thinking: it's one breath of mine against three of hers,
That's what our rhythm seems to be.

I hear this couple talking,
Two voices modulating into one,
Softly speaking spectres of promise.

I spy on her asleep
Sensing a child in her with too many dreams
To chose from, her jaws clenched
To keep them inside till they rot
While she dies slowly in her sleep.

Casual chords coming from open car windows
Signalling to me that these are New York symphonies
And also: that Elise is still here, with me,
That I must write for her.

Her eyes closed in the half-light,
A film of cold sweat on her pale skin,
Her neck exposed to my murderous mind,
And me slicing through her sighs
While all I feel is music, my music melting
In the smothering air we breathe, one against three.

She came to me. Her mouth
Full of crunched-up words,
A meaningless alphabet to her tune.
She turns her slender body away

So I can wipe it dry and write,
Write on her bony back, as on a blackboard,
Feeling the whipping flame on my eyes
When I see too much of her
And want to write, my love, my love,
But instead I write two notes – *ta – ta*
A diminished second, and from there: on.

This I will hear until I go deaf
And then it will last.

Two notes dancing in a ripped-up dawn,
I, sadly, take to my formal clothes, a composer again,
My mind still playing with the thought of her body
Gasping – *ta – ta* – while I brush my hair,
Reacquire my intense stare.
Her glow on me in the mirror,

It is her planet I live on,
Nothing belongs to me but music.

I bring broken notebooks.
Winging my way down to the New York subway,
My history in my shaking hands.

The entrance is like a gargoyle upside-down.
I dive into its steam-spouting mouth,
My pores oozing fear.
I walked this score.
I see, I can hear
The mini masters who play my music have sorted me out
While they keep talking about Elise and me,
Hammering out her tune – *ta – ta.*

I am inside the whale, in my ears, in my heart
Wanting to fight against the pulse – *ta – ta.*
But it's here, played on a steel drum
Beet – Beethoven on a pot, a drum looking like
A caved-in reproduction of our gutted earth,
A rivulet of my music, my feelings scored.
This tender tone: for Elise.
Ta – ta – ta – ta – ta from there: onwards.
And they say I have Asperger Syndrome.

JOHN MONTAGUE

A Holy Vision

I saw a tiny Christ
caper on the cross

silent as a salamander
writhing in fire or

a soldier triumphant
when the battle's lost;

wine bursts from
his body's grapeskin:

'The suffering you see
is our daily mystery,

so follow my body
as it sings mutely

(a lantern, a ladder,
a window, a pathway)

of pain calcined away
in a dance of ecstasy.'

SINÉAD MORRISSEY

The Old Zoo

Most provocative in winter –
when the trees along the Antrim Road
have thinned to their own frail vascular systems,
abjectly symmetrical, and any passing passenger
travelling west to the city centre
in sporadic flashes and for seconds at a stretch can catch
what's left of the old zoo,
rising on the right
like a *trompe l'oeil* flourish
or a trick from the Arabian Nights.

Abandoned over a decade ago,
it thrusts and rots.
Dead leaves at the Bellevue bus-stop stop up its throat.
A woman fell asleep
and about her grew a thicket
of hay-bale wires and briars, huts
for the animals with their roofs
caved-in, a few more generous enclosures,
oddly suspended on the Cave Hill's incline, a tin-
can bandstand and a rusted turnstile

two rollerbooted girls passed through
in 1986, having skated miles
and faced a wall of rain to get here on their own.
The big cats paced, psychotic,
in their row of concrete cages
and a brown bear covered its eyes.

Snowy parakeets,
ingeniously trapped inside a staked-up net,
sang out for England
and War with France.

Now the animals measure out their wider houses
closer to the summit,
and none of them stare through bars.
The old zoo keeps its offices –
its stacked and emptied terraces
of grass and space, its windowless
out-buildings – all standing
to attention like a choir of Mennonites.
If you laid your head down on its tangled flank,
you'd sleep, also.

PAUL MURRAY

In the End

That they know it
or not, that we
know it or not
is not important.
What matters is
that all of us, all
of them, lovers
and madmen, mothers
and sad men – all
sing from a wound.

NUALA NÍ CHONCHÚIR

My Name is William Clongallen

MY NAME IS GUILLERMO DANTE and the woman who I called mama did not give birth to me. It wasn't until my papa died that mama told me who I was. I knew I looked different – my brothers couldn't let me forget; in a family of dark-skinned boys, I alone was pale-eyed and fair. Mama used to say it was because I was sickly, but I never felt anything but robust. She kept me home with her to do my lessons, though I longed to join the others at the Good Shepherd School on Brown Street. My brothers called me *mamalón* – mama's boy – until she whacked at their backsides with her broom and they ran screeching. All of Brooklyn belonged to my brothers while I, it seemed, belonged only to mama.

I was twelve years old when mama took me to Alejandro's Café to tell me about my mother. Alejandro came out from the kitchen to sympathise with us over papa.

'He was a good man, Selena; a great man.'

'*Muchas gracias*, Alejandro,' mama said and patted his hand. Alejandro shook and he swiped at tears; it was as if he was the one with a dead husband. Mama thanked him again and ordered coffee for herself and ice-cream for me. Alejandro shuffled away.

'Guillermo,' mama said to me, 'there is something you should know. It is a sad story but you must not cry.'

'I won't cry, mama,' I said, though I wasn't sure whether I would or not. I had cried over papa but not too much; I was never a favourite of his, like Primo, my eldest brother.

A waiter came over and served mama's coffee and my ice-cream.

'Do you remember papa told you that he made a great sea trip when you were a baby?'

'He sailed from New York to Spain and then all the way back to New York again.'

'That's right. Well, that ship that papa sailed on stopped at an island called Ireland on its voyage back.'

Mama's face was serious and I didn't like it; I suckled ice-cream off my spoon and eyed her.

'Ireland?' I said.

'Yes. And there the boat picked up many people including a poor young woman and her baby boy. Papa, being a kind man, saw that the woman was having troubles so he helped her and the baby, but she was very, very ill and she died on board. Her name was Mary Carter.'

'Mary Carter,' I repeated, wondering if I was supposed to cry because the woman was dead. 'Did we know Mary Carter, mama? Was she one of us?'

'You knew her, Guillermo, and she knew you.' Mama leaned forward and gripped my fingers. 'She was your real mama, *mi amor*.' Then she began to sob and Alejandro came over and put his hand on her shoulder. Everyone in the café stared while pretending not to. I looked at the lid of mama's coffee pot which, because it didn't close properly, seemed to smile at me.

Mama waved Alejandro away and continued to speak. 'Mary Carter was buried at sea. Papa took charge of her baby – you – and changed your name from William to Guillermo. He carried you home to me in Brooklyn. Papa brought nothing of Mary's; he did not even take the blanket you were wrapped in.'

Mama shook her head and went on to say that papa told her all he knew about my mother: that she was from the County of Limerick in Ireland and she had lived in a house called Clongallen with the Cookes. That was all. He forbade mama to tell me about myself, but she wanted me to know and she took her chance as soon as papa was cooling in his grave.

Before we married, I told Rosita about Mary Carter. I wanted her to know that I wasn't who I appeared to be, though, as I explained to her, I felt fully like myself.

'You must go to Ireland, *mi amor*, and see where you are from,' she said, excited; 'see who your mother was.'

'I'm from Brooklyn, Rosita, and mama was all the mother I needed.'

'Guillermo, you are Irish by birth. That means something.'

'I am American,' I said, ending the matter.

But the same conversation was repeated over the years as we reared our family of girls; it was always Rosita who started it, with a shy, angry look that meant I was being reproached. I tamped down any gnawing thoughts of Mary Carter and, to my wife, proclaimed her irrelevant. It wasn't until our eldest daughter had a baby boy, and I saw his helpless, beautiful form, that I felt the need to find out about my birthplace.

I held my grandson up to my wife and said, 'Now I am ready. Now I will go.'

Rosita was afraid of aeroplanes, so I flew alone to Ireland in search of Mary Carter's life. It was a cheerless country. Brooklyn has its share of rain, cold and dark but Ireland was swamped in drizzle and drear from the moment I arrived to the moment I left. I wondered how the people could stand it and I could see why Mary had taken a way out.

I landed at Shannon airport and within minutes was driving alongside green fields dotted with cows and sheep, their muzzles fixed to the grass in an eternity of grazing. The rain sluiced onto the car and I drove, hunched over the steering wheel, alert to road signs, afraid I would lose my way. I cursed Rosita for making me come to this place; I cursed Mary Carter for being Irish; I cursed the rain.

I spent the night in a guesthouse called Emerald Sunrise; I lay rigid in the bed and slept in half hour snatches. In the morning, the bleak-faced landlord gave me directions and stood at the door to watch me drive away as if I were the last guest he might ever take in.

Clongallen House looked derelict. It sat high above the surrounding countryside, at the end of an unmade road; its walls were streaked and the windows were shuttered. The grounds were a tangle of bushes and weeds. I parked the car and stood in front of the house: it had been a grand place once, I thought. I walked around the back and saw a light. I knocked at the window and an old woman looked out; I waved, feeling foolish. She unlatched the door.

'Yes?' she said.

'Hullo! My name is Guillermo Dante and I am looking for the man of the house. A Mr Cooke?'

'There's no one by that name here,' she said, and started to close the door.

'I've come all the way from Brooklyn, New York,' I said, stepping forward.

The old woman looked at me. 'Well, you're at the wrong place, Sir.'

I wanted to keep her talking. 'It's a gloomy day, Ma'am,' I said, sticking my hand out to catch the rain.

'Maybe you brought your own gloom,' she said and shut the door.

I stood for a few moments then got back into the car and drove down the overgrown avenue to the small road that lead up to the gates. I travelled for a mile or so and stopped at a pub called Harty's – its lights looked warm through the misty rain. There were a few elderly men at the bar; I took a low seat under a glass box that housed a plump pheasant perched on dead grass.

The barmaid shouted over, 'What will you have?' I looked at the men who were drinking and pointed. 'A bottle of stout,' the barmaid said.

The telephone rang as the barmaid put the glass and bottle in front of me, cutting short whatever she was about to say. She was soon back.

'It's for you,' she said.

I looked up at her. 'What's for me, Ma'am?'

'The 'phone,' she said, as if I were half mad.

I was sure she was mistaken but I got up anyway and followed her into a back kitchen which smelt sour, like cabbage water. I lifted the receiver.

'Hullo?'

'Come up tomorrow,' said a voice.

'I beg your pardon?'

'Come up to Clongallen in the morning and we'll talk.' It was the old woman from the house.

'How did you know I'd be here?' I said.

'Sure where else would you be?' she said and hung up.

I drove back to the Emerald Sunrise and the landlord acted as if he had never met me before; I stayed in the same room I had been in the previous night and, this time, I slept well.

⁀

'What business have you here?' the old woman said, accepting the bunch of roses I handed her and tossing them onto a chair. I had driven to the city and back to buy them. She pointed to a fireside couch and I sat down.

'I understand my birth mother lived here once,' I said. 'My name is Guillermo Dante but I was christened William. My mother was called Mary Carter. Or Cooke, I'm not sure.'

She studied me. 'There was no one called Cooke here, I told you that. You'll have tea.' She filled a black kettle at a deep sink.

'And your own name, Ma'am?'

'Never mind my name. I was the cook for the family here. There's hardly a one of them left. What remains are beyond in England.'

'Did you happen to know Mary Carter?'

'I knew her. She was a bold girl and a good girl all in the one sack. She broke her own mother's heart.'

The kettle grunted on the hob and the woman tossed some biscuits onto a plate. She sat on a kitchen chair in front of me and folded her hands in her lap.

'Did she break her mother's heart by leaving for the United States?'

She leaned forward. 'By opening her legs to a man who'd never marry her.'

The woman got up suddenly and made tea, stirring the pot lavishly before placing it where the kettle had been. I felt embarrassed, for myself and for her. I wasn't thirsty but I would drink the tea as she had made it. She rose again, poured and handed me a cup.

'Thank you,' I said and took a sip. The woman stood over me, watching.

'Follow me,' she said.

I looked at the teacup in my hand but she was already unlatching a door on the other side of the room, so I left it down and went after her. I walked behind her up a freezing staircase. Up and up we went, drawing the mildewed air into our lungs; the cold was cloying, it felt like hands pulling at my face. She stopped at a door in a corridor and I stood beside her, breathing raggedly after the long ascent. Opening the door, she gestured for me to go in. I dipped under the lintel and stood in a tiny, empty room with a low roof.

'You were born in this room,' the woman said.

I whipped around and stared at her. She nodded. I surveyed the dim space; the floorboards were grey and runnels of water had made one wall green. I could hear rain thrashing down on the roof.

'This is the attic,' I said.

'Mary Carter was a servant in this house. Our master, Lord Clongallen, took advantage of her and ... well, I delivered you myself.' She squeezed my arm.

'Mary died on the boat crossing to New York.'

The woman gasped and blessed herself. 'No!' she said. 'God be good to her.'

She bent her head and let a low groan, so I held her elbow and we made our way back down the stairs. Our tea had cooled but I put a cup into her hands and she drank. Tears dropped from her eyes and she pushed them away with her sleeve.

'I wondered why I never heard from Mary. I thought she might write; one letter even, to let me know she was safe. God help me, I'm responsible for her death.'

'I doubt it, Ma'am. How could that be?'

'I encouraged her to go. I gave her the fare.'

'You couldn't have known she would take ill,' I said.

'The master and his missus were going to keep Baby William – you – for their own; it wasn't right. You were Mary's child, first and forever.'

'Yes,' I said.

'I should have seen her right. The peteen,' the old woman said. She told me the little she knew about Mary – that she was fourteen years old; that she came from Pallaskenry, a village west of the city of Limerick. She said I looked like Mary but I wasn't sure if she meant it.

'Oh, sure you're the spit of her. I knew it last night.'

'Was she a nice person?' I said. 'You mentioned she was "bold".'

'Mary Carter was lively and had her own mind. She loved children, she certainly did.' The woman smiled. 'Mary was a brazen strip, if you really want to know.'

'Geez,' I said and laughed.

'You have sisters, three of them. The master's girls. They all live in Suffolk in England, they don't come here.'

I nodded and thought about that; I couldn't see how meeting them would make better anything about me or my life. I rose from the chair and offered her my hand.

'Will you tell me your name now?' I said.

She shook her head. 'No. But I can tell you yours: your name is Lord William Clongallen.' She hugged me suddenly. 'God speed, William,' she said, walking me to the door.

I stood outside in the mizzle that drenched the countryside; I stretched my arms over my head and shouted to the sky, 'My name is William Clongallen.' I took a deep breath. 'My name is William Clongallen,' I roared.

A pigeon broke from a tree and futtered skywards before landing on a higher branch. I got into the car and sat for a few moments, staring at the land, the rain, the slate sky; I longed to be home in Brooklyn. The journey before me looked endless. I rested my forehead on the steering wheel then sat up straight.

'My name is Guillermo Dante,' I said and started the engine and drove away.

EILÉAN NÍ CHUILLEANÁIN

Judgement Day

For once, here's a subject where no corner is left
For a cat or a lion, there's no shelf
For a parked cardinal's hat, no neat
Stack of wood for winter, no tools
Tidy on their hooks.
                                  Nobody calmly
Pouring wine or hoisting a weighty barrel,
Not even a window or a door to admit
Light from a garden or a bare yard –
Only rising bodies and falling, and odd blown scraps,
Or bolts unrolling, of coloured cloths,
Wide falls or skimped ends.
                                  The robed
Processions of my childhood that wound past
Open doors with hallstands, area gates,
Narrow entries pointing, curving,
Wisely departing cats
                                  – Is this
Where they were bound, this great quarrel where
Nothing is real, only the teeth and the bite
And the cascading remnants that curtain away what has passed,
The shod feet that have rounded
The corner by now, and muffle
The voices to which in any case
No heed is paid, intoning their single note?

NUALA NÍ DHOMHNAILL

An Bhatráil

Thugas mo leanbhán liom aréir ón lios
ar éigean.
Bhí sé lán suas de mhíola is de chnathacha
is a chraiceann chomh smiotaithe is chomh gargraithe
go bhfuilim ó mhaidin ag cur ceiríní teo lena thóin
is ag cuimilt *Sudocrem* dá chabhail
ó bhonn a choise go clár a éadain.

Trí bhanaltra a bhí aige ann
is deoch bhainne tugtha ag beirt acu dó.
Dá mbeadh an tríú duine acu tar éis tál air
bheadh deireach go deo agam leis.
Bhíodar á chaitheamh go neamheaglach
ó dhuine go chéile,
á chur ó láimh go láimh, ag rá
'Seo mo leanbhsa, chughat do leanbhsa.
Seo mo leanbhsa, chughat do leanbhsa.'

Thángas eatarthu isteach de gheit
is ruas ar chiotóg air.
Thairrigíos trí huaire é tré urla an tsnáith ghlais
a bhí i mo phóca agam.
Nuair a tháinig an fear caol dubh romham
ag doras an leasa
dúrt leis an áit a fhágaint láithreach
nó go sáfainn é.
Thugas faobhar na scine coise duibhe
don sceach a bhí sa tslí
romham is a dhá cheann i dtalamh aige.

Bhuel, tá san go maith is níl go holc.
Tá fíor na croise bainte agam
as tlú na tine
is é builte trasna an chliabháin agam.
Is má chuireann siad aon rud eile nach liom
isteach ann
an diabhal ná gurb é an chaor dhearg
a gheobhaidh sé!
Chaithfinn é a chur i ngort ansan.
Níl aon seans riamh go bhféadfainn dul in aon ghaobhar
d'aon ospidéal leis.
Mar atá
beidh mo leordhóthain dalladh agam
ag iarraidh a chur in iúl dóibh
nach mise a thug an bhatráil dheireanach seo dó.

The Battering

I only just made it home last night with my child
from the fairy fort.
He was crawling with lice and jiggers
and his skin was so red and raw
I've spent all day putting hot poultices on his bottom
and salving him with Sudocrem
from stem to stern.

Of the three wet-nurses back in the fort,
two had already suckled him:
had he taken so much as a sip from the third
that's the last I'd have seen of him.
As it was, they were passing him around
with such recklessness,

one to the next, intoning,
'Little laddie to me, to you little laddie.
Laddie to me, la di da, to you laddie.'

I came amongst them all of a sudden
and caught him by his left arm.
Three times I drew him through the land of undid wool
I'd been carrying in my pocket.
When a tall, dark stranger barred my way
at the door of the fort
I told him to get off-side fast
or I'd run him through.
The next obstacle was a briar,
both ends of which were planted in the ground:
I cut it with my trusty black-handled knife.

So far, so good.
I've made the sign of the cross
with the tongs
and laid them on the cradle.
If they try to sneak anything past
that's not my own, if they try to pull another fast
one on me, it won't stand a snowball's
chance in hell:
I'd have to bury it out in the field.
There's no way I could take it anywhere next
or near the hospital.
As things stand,
I'll have more than enough trouble
trying to convince them that it wasn't me
who gave my little laddie this last battering.

translated by Paul Muldoon

JEAN O'BRIEN

On The Line

Our train from Edinburgh delayed
by a death on the line, I recalled
that girl who knelt on a track
hands joined as if in prayer, and I'd read how
the driver never drove another train,
said he would see her forever
at the moment of impact as he screamed
to an unheeding God and the wheels skidded
on the iron tracks. At last we were underway,
this lost time a slight annoyance in our day
soon given over to the healing sight of
fast moving coastline.

Small inlets flanked by headlands
gave glimpses down to the sea,
waves juddering on the pebble beach.
A hawk holds itself still in the thermals
its wingspan two hands splayed
visually tracking its prey, almost in line
with our window, as he hovers over sea-spray;
then, as if we were derailed
an unexpected tunnel cuts the light in two,
just as suddenly we emerged and journeyed on.

Pulling out of Newcastle I glanced up
from my book and saw wooden wings
thrown wide, Angel of the North,
Gormley's angel holding its own on a hillside
in stinging rain and buffeting winds
casting its shadow deep.

We speed on in a blur of fields, sea and sky
and wondered where exactly
on this track did someone choose today
to die, while we waited for the end of the line.

JOSEPH O'CONNOR

Pontius Pilate as an Old Man Exiled to France

For years after his crucifixion, I did not think of him.
Preoccupied, sand-blown, by what came next.
My demotion, relocation – I'm not sure of the term.
Latin is subtle. My decentralisation.

They say he was born at the close of the year.
His followers I mean; they rumour of him still.
The fools do not realise a wintertime child
Is always unlucky, will be forgotten in the end.

I missed Palestine for a while. The girls
There were beautiful. But what matters that
At the death of a career? Thirty years'
Service rinsed away in a hot moment.

My wife did not come with me here. We had lost
Our cadence. And she'd never liked me much.
My touch did not content her; I was fat
By then, did not contest the divorce.

She was kind to our sons. I cannot gripe.
I simply wasn't the marrying type.

She lives back in Rome; a government villa
In the red loamy hills – the gardens there are pleasant –
By the cedar forest close to the Via Rugalla
Where we hotly courted once. But it doesn't

Do to fix on the past. 'Time's a river'
Wrote Heraclitus. It can't be re-crossed.

I think of her sometimes. I'll never
See her again. And my children, too, are lost.

So that really, now, there is only work
To fill up the days and the sleeting nights.
I don't complain. It's worthy of remark
How exiles always have limited rights.

She ignores my sometime letters. Perhaps it is best.
When a marriage has died, it is wiser laid to rest ...

And the natives, these Gauls – they could be worse.
My soldiers report that they are obedient, clean,
Understand what is expected. Of course
They do not love us, because they have seen
Our capability, know we are strict;
But a modus vivendi has been reached
By now: I demand that any edict
Be totally observed -- but if approached
I can be reasonable, will give ear
To a case. They already know they're crushed.

No point in humiliation when fear
Is enough. It is folly to grind them.
Better to promulgate bright future days,
The bad years of liberty long behind them.

I am safe in most of the city when I walk at night –
(Caesar, in Rome, could you boast half as much?)
I crucify few, show discretion, reduce taxes,
Torture but rarely, water-board their thieves.
My administration has brought peace, they are not hungry
Any more. And yet – it is strange – they look
At me resentfully, like crocodiles
Up to their snouts in some famished swamp.

Guile in the glances of their children, too;
The patient serenity of their hatred.

I rise in the dark, attempt lyrics, odes,
The scratch of my nib on the lamb-skin vellum.
The dawn-lit rite damps down my sleepless thoughts,
This desk a kind of raft to which I grip;
Its inks and quills; the serpents of its scrolls;
Its small bust of Caesar; its map of Judea.

And he comes to me, then. In the night,
Like a ghost. In this last cold month
Of the year, he always comes.
The season of his birth, so his followers whisper,
When the glister of the ice makes the lake
A place of dangers, and the snow wolves
Haunt the bins of the city.

I sense him in mist, in steam, in the frost
That glitters dead cornfields in wintertime.
In rainstorms, in hail, in the bowl in which I wash,
In the water I shave with, the ice in my wine.
I taste him in the empty and snow-muffled squares,
In the spittle of my mouth, in my blood when I am cut;
In the strange tears I weep, in my sweat when I dread
The Via Doloroso of an empty bed.

And my thirst is a dredger, my cud a cake of salt,
Unquenchable nights in the wringing, ruined sheets
That shackle my limbs. Is it now my fault
I granted the abasement you appeared to seek?
I bathe in him, drink him – can never be free.
Gods – *Gods* – You have abandoned me.

I see him in snowfields, the slow thaw of his victory
Dripping from icicles; I crunch him in puddles.
My bread tastes of sweat, my wine of blood;
He flakes in my palm when a hailstone smacks my skin.
'Leave me,' I mumble, 'for pity, let me be –'
And my bodyguards believe I am speaking to them.

All those years I did not think of him. Hardly at all.
Would never grant him anchor in the Tiber of the mind;
For I did as duty needed. *I followed my orders.*
A problem needs solutions. Are you crazy? Blind?
Then run to your vagrant! See if he heals.
'Forgiveness?' 'Mercy?' These are words for little girls.
'Give your coat to your brother'? 'Help the frail'? 'Love the poor'?
Political correctness gone mad; nothing more.

He was a misfit who heard voices;
A moon-child; I pitied him;
A butt of jokes; a baby; not a man of the world.
A tramp born in a pigsty, in the reeking filth and cold.
He will soon be forgotten. And I will grow old.
And they will see I did my duty,
A beautiful thing.
And they will honour *me* then,
In the closing of the year,
When water freezes over,
Until snowdrops appear
And cows are led from dark stables,
Stupefied by sunlight.
And my hands will again be clean
As winter.

MARY O'DONOGHUE

My Daughter in Winter Costume

after John Axelrod's sculpture (1922)

She is sealed like a bomb in her anorak.
Her face is flushed fruit under the hood.
She's already moving away. I want to call her back.

At nine in the morning the sky is blue-black.
I think of hard falls, split lips, her blood.
But she's sealed like a bomb in her anorak,

and shouting to friends on the tarmac,
a yardful of children, a tide, a flood
already moving away. I want to call her back,

I'm faint, suddenly starved with the lack
of her, and determined that she should
know, all sealed like a bomb in her anorak.

Grip the wheel. Radio on. The yakety-yak
of today's talking heads on How to Be Good.
The morning is moving away. I want to call her back.

This is what it's like to be left slack,
the cord frayed like I knew it would.
She is sealed like a bomb in her anorak,
already moved away, and I can't call her back.

JOHN O'DONNELL

Hoppers

Jeez your hands are freezing –
his big paws slobbering all over,
struggling to hold her squirming
underneath him, gleaming silver prize
he'd scooped out of the water, one

we always knew would get away, escape
the fish tin jongling down the street, tied
to the Just-Married car we'd waved off
at the hotel and gathered round again
as sweating rescue workers hauled metal

dripping from the river and tried to prise
the locked doors open. Two the pine
but ten to raise the oak, she following
behind them down the aisle in tight new
widow's weeds. *His greatest ever catch,*

the best man had said, to laughter; her,
and the tiddler son they'd landed a year later.
He'd taught that boy everything: the pitch
and flick of casting, how to watch for stirrings
on the rod, and how to bait the line

with hoppers captured in long grass,
buzz and scurry in an airless jar, clarets,
ambers, pearlies, pierced to hide the hook;
how beauty at first tempts and then reveals
its barbed surprise. How to wait, drowsy

by the river dreaming of tight lines, or sleepless
under night skies filled with planes he'd thought
were stars, awaiting her return from far upriver,
spawning elsewhere with another, glitter of
her still-damp scales and of her tears

when she'd said she wanted out. But he'd
reeled in bigger ones before, ones looking
to escape the net; all it took was patience,
he told himself, loading carefully the car
for the last time, rods and reels stashed in

beside the anxious child; patience, and the right bait.
Accidental, the coroner declared, though the road
straight and the bridge over the river wide; and why
anyway, why, unless slow arc of the car through air
his final cast, offering to the river his firstborn

like ancients desperate for a fair harvest or rain,
as if love were a greedy fish unable to resist
the lure strapped into the back seat, rising open-jawed
from reed-choked gloom to snatch away
this life, so short, so bright, so sweet.

MARY O'DONNELL

Lifting Skin

THE DAY AFTER HER ARRIVAL, a Dublin family pulled up just when she had settled her things on the desk at the open window. Outdoorsy and slim, like people in an ad for breakfast cereals, they unstrapped two prawn-like infants from their car-seats, then made their noisy way into the terraced holiday home beside hers. Although they weren't particularly friendly, that suited Dervla, and she waved at them each day as she pulled away in the car, smiling without stopping to chat. Rain or shine, she wore square, soot-black Dior sunglasses that had cost nearly half a month's salary – big square beautiful frames, perfect for Cannes, too glamorous for Carrigbwee. The next-door mother often sat in her sun-porch, herself wearing fashion shades, a mobile phone clamped to her ear as her infants played. Her pale blonde, very silky hair slid over both shoulders. Unconsciously, Dervla adjusted her own glasses. A public nurse visiting an elderly neighbour back in Dublin had stopped her the previous week right on the street – enquiring in the gentle but not judgemental voice of a caring professional, if everything was *all right*. Now, down by the coast, she didn't want to spark misguided interest. She would drive around the cliff road to Neptune Bay, dipping into a tunnelling laneway, down more steeply still to the bluff above the beach.

By the time the third week arrived, her routine was impregnable. Neptune Bay was safe, she thought. The sand was coarse enough to ensure it would never be popular with the families that clustered on the yellow beach nearer the village. Here, she could be alone. She was thankful for the four month break from the department of Celtic Studies. Not only could she sit it out for these weeks, but she was making progress on a paper provisionally called *The Celts in the Iberian Peninsula*. Work on the myths of identity and history seemed a far cry from what was going on beneath her face, as it healed from recent cosmetic surgery of the drastic kind – a full yanking up of jaw-line and sagging cheeks, the removal of bags from beneath frank, intelligent eyes, the fine slicing away of the hooded skin above them. To ensure that the banner of beauty could fly once again, she'd even let them raise her brow-line. She would return to the academic fold in late September, newly minted – she hoped – with the illusion of youthfulness making her glow. The same, only different.

It was not the kind of topic that got much of an airing in the Common Room, where the Marys of her generation sometimes exchanged survival notes. These children of the mid-Fifties were not *all* called Mary, but she considered most of them to be Mary-like. Máire from Gweedore had recently adopted a Vietnamese baby girl. It was the talk of the department, and discussion behind her back ranged from admiration to one or two traditional comments on how motherhood would clip her wings. Muireann in Folklore was in the middle of a divorce, and Mairín was the mother of four teenagers. They discussed these subjects with one another, carefully and caringly, usually in the absence of their male colleagues.

Dervla had not mentioned the facelift to anybody apart from her husband Dan. Why would she need to do such a thing, he wondered aloud when she told him of her intention, his eyes widening.

Because, she replied.

'You think it's silly and pathetic,' she added.

He touched her arm. ' I just don't understand …'

For a moment she said nothing.

'Maybe I don't understand either. It's just … I don't want to look … *old …*'

'Well,' he shrugged, 'if it won't turn you into one of those rubber-faced freaks, why not?'

It had been very straightforward. Local anaesthetic throughout, face numbed as the surgeon marked and outlined, chatting away to the anaesthetist. She had watched him raise his delicate lacerating instruments, and with every fine, painless tug, felt herself being re-created. The youth and radiance still within her, pushed more closely to the surface of not-yet-old skin. She could feel it in her healing epidermis, dancing to get out.

From what she absorbed in her twilit state, both doctors spent as much time as possible down in Schull. As the surgeon gently tugged or, in the case of her eyes, cut and cauterised, she sensed the ease of men at work and at play and, to her surprise, she despised them. Mostly though, she despised herself for needing them.

Another week passed and still she drove to Neptune Bay. Dan was in Kerry, climbing Carrantoohill. They sent idiotic, comically-cryptic texts to one another, for their eyes only. Their two daughters were in Mexico, learning Spanish. She wondered if they'd notice the difference in her when they returned to UCC in the autumn. She stood in the warm July sun, face slathered in sunblock, watching the horizon through her sunglasses. If she sailed straight on she would arrive at Finisterre, the end of the earth for the ancients, but the start of Galicia, in north-western Spain.

Three weeks after the operation, she was starting to resemble her old self. The slightly mashed and swollen bruising had subsided. What remained was an Asian yellowness and residual patches of blood beneath her eyes that had yet to be absorbed. With make-up, camouflage would be possible within the next few days. Satisfied, she turned the key in the ignition and pulled away from the beach.

The cottage was overheated when she got back. She flung the front windows wide and sat down at the table, laptop open. The infants next door were screaming their heads off, but the half-written article awaited her attention. She stopped for a moment, listening again. It was the woman's voice, calling out, it seemed. She leaned forward slightly and peered out the window. The man was leaving in a great hurry. He stepped into the four-by-four, shut the door smartly, then snorted off down the village street. She began to tap at the keyboard, and the next sentence came easily. An urgent rapping at the door disturbed her.

'Fuck!' she said between her teeth, not bothering to lean out the window to see who it was. She strode towards the hall door and pulled it open. The woman from next door practically fell into the hall, bubbles of blood beading a split lower lip. Her mouth opened soundlessly for a moment, revealing blood-vivid teeth. The nose was skewed sideways and also bled. The skin beneath one eye was livid though not broken.

'Sorry to bother you ...'

The thick, fluid-choked voice gave out and again she struggled to speak.

'It's the children. Can't leave . . . ' Then she screamed, and more metallic-smelling blood ruptured in clots and bubbles from her nose, spraying out onto Dervla who could not stop staring, even as she reached for the woman's arm and drew her into the sitting-room. She got the woman to sit and tried to control her own horror. As she dialled the doctor with one hand, she held on to the woman's arm with the other, as if she was a child who might escape her grip. The doctor's number was engaged.

'Tell me your name.'

The woman wiped her mouth.

'M-m-*ma-*,' she mumbled.

'What's that?' Dervla asked, leaning close.

The woman drew in a breath and pushed the word out.

'Em-maa! ... Em-ma! ... *Emma!* ...' she repeated, as if she had just learned who she really was. Dervla took a tissue from her jeans pocket. It was clean. She reached out as if to dab beneath the woman's nostrils. But she pulled back and mumbled something Dervla couldn't pick up.

'Leave it – it needs to dry up itself.'

So this wasn't the first time.

'I'm going to make tea before we go. Sweet tea before you go anywhere, Emma,' she insisted, not sure if she was doing the right thing or not. Emma nodded compliantly, began wiping around her lips with her T-shirt. They were swollen and purple.

'Who did this to you?' Dervla asked softly. The answer was obvious of course, and rage rose from her gut, so violent she wanted to explode. Emma said nothing.

For a moment, the other woman struggled to straighten her shoulders, to hold herself erect, as if to say she still had some pride, some coating of protective, womanly deception at her disposal. But just as quickly, she slumped forward and gave up.

'My husband,' she whispered, and began to cry. It wasn't loud crying. It was a miserable, despairing sort of snivel, what should really have been a full-on Medusa-like bellow. For a moment Dervla said nothing. What she wanted to do was put her arms around Emma and just hold her. Maybe rock her, as one would an injured child. But she didn't.

'Emma? Are the kids alone now?'

Emma nodded.

'I'd better go to them. Emma?'

The other woman looked up, as if seeing her for the first time. Again she nodded.

'Yes. Get them please. Bring them to me.'

The kettle was boiling. Dervla leaned down and put her arm around Emma's shoulder as much as she dared. Some of the blood was smeared into her blondeness, around her hairline, running around the edges of her face and down towards her left ear-lobe. She hardly knew what to say, yet wanted to say something. Incredibly, Emma was already pulling herself together, she could feel it, an endurance of some kind. The trembling had stopped, the crying had stopped. Even the blood from her nose was now thickening on her face. Soon it would start to dry.

'Emma – I'm so sorry that this is happening to you . . . '

She chided herself for feeling inarticulate, for not knowing either what to do or what to say. Tea. What use was tea? As Dervla moved to go and collect the children, Emma caught her arm.

'And you? How did *that* happen?' She pointed to Dervla's face, a puzzled, concerned expression in her eyes. Of course. She wasn't wearing the sunglasses. It was clear what Emma was thinking.

'Oh I'll tell you about that in a minute!' she said lightly, fleeing next door to gather up the babies who were roaring for their mother. She wondered what to tell Emma, how to answer her perfectly reasonable question. If she believed in karma or the cosmos sending little niggling messages, this would be one long memo. It was unfair. One face mashed by a Bad Bastard Husband, another's voluntarily mashed, and Good Husband innocently scaling Carrantoohill, letting her get on with a life that seemed more vapid by the minute.

DENNIS O'DRISCOLL

Say But The Word

You eat your ill-judged
    words in the early
hours, take them back,

retract them one by one,
    try to erase the memory,
remove all trace,

arrive at more benign
    interpretations:
some form of words

to set your stressed-out
    mind at rest,
broker a truce with

your unyielding self,
    allow you draft terms
you could sleep on,

leaving the record blank
    as the crumpled sheets
you toss between.

           ⌒

Say the word 'Future':
    you despatch it to the past.

Say the word 'Silence':
  you undo it.

Say the word 'Nothing':
  you make something of it.

[*after Wislawa Szymborska*]

❧

Phone home urgently.
  The power of simple words.
You never forget.

❧

So many of the things
  we go in fear of most
may never happen.

We fear them all the more
  the more they keep
not happening.

❧

Where there's life
there's hope.

Hope and despair.

Despair because
we can but hope.

MICHAEL O'LOUGHLIN

An excerpt from **The Jewish Bride**

Amsterdam, 1664

T HEY BROUGHT HER TO HIM on the night following a grey spring day, when his mood was blacker than usual. He had sneezed and coughed all through the winter in his room crawling with damp. It was biting cold and the grey sky pressed down like a lid on the city. Fragments of dirty ice still floated on the canals and the streets were a quagmire. It was not the clean, healthy winter in Oran, with the light beating off the blue sea, and the hot sun of Africa, and he found himself remembering more often the warmth of his lost birthplace.

Sasportas laid down his pen. In the room bare but for bed and lectern, there was a small shelf which contained a few precious books, and writing materials. Near his right hand lay his copy of the Zohar, the Book of Splendour. He picked up the book and felt with an almost sensuous pleasure the worn Spanish leather of its binding. This book had accompanied him everywhere like a faithful servant, like a bride even, for was it not written that the Shekhinath is the bride of knowledge?

Outside his room, in a tall, narrow house on a poor Jewish street near the Amstel, all was quiet. The city had halted its mad rush for business for a few necessary hours of rest, and merchants lay twitching in their bedsteads dreaming of gold. Moonlight lit up the quiet canals where not a boat moved at this hour. A drunken Dutchman sang an obscene song as he staggered along. Often they fell in and drowned and lent their stink to the city air. Some were never found, and sometimes bodies would lie on the bottom, to surface months later, swollen, rotten, fish-eaten.

He took up his pen and continued to write:

'So know that the only way is the way of the Law. It is only by strict adherence to the Law that the day of Redemption can be hastened and the Jewish people...'

He cursed as a knock came to the door. Without asking for permission his insolent servant girl stepped in and told him there were some Jews to see him. Behind her a crowd of poor Jews wailed and rocked and pushed their way into his room, loudly proclaiming his wisdom, his holiness, his erudition. Out of their shouted meanderings he had finally understood that they wanted him to talk to a girl, though the reason still escaped him. They mumbled something about madness, blasphemy, unclean spirits. Did they take him for some kind of exorcist? Did they think he would mumble some phrases from the kabbalah and charge them a guilder for the service?

He couldn't get an answer as to what her affliction was. Why him? Surely she should have been brought to the parnasim, to the elders, the learned rabbis? But he had already become a presence in the city. The synagogue officials, the fawning Portuguese curs, were civil and paid him a stipend from the community fund. But they kept him at arm's length. He was not their sort. No, it was the common people who were most impressed by him, they knew he was a cabbalist, though they did not even know what that was. They thought him some kind of magician, as he strode the narrow streets in his long dark cloak and his beard already grey. The servant girl had dared to speak to him one day, looking him full in the face without lowering her eyes, and with an offensive levity asked him if it was true that a cabbalist could create a man from clay? Sasportas admonished her for blasphemy. Only G-d could create a man. Blushing, she mumbled something about asking G-d to create one for her and flounced out.

Exasperated, he nodded assent and like a group of guilty schoolchildren they had drawn back and pushed the girl forward. She was wrapped in a green cloak, with her black hair pushing out from under a scarf, her gesture at modesty. With a gesture he dismissed them and praying, thanking, bowing, praising, they left, probably to huddle against his door outside so as not to miss a thing.

The girl stood there before him and raised her eyes to his. Sasportas had little experience of these matters, but he knew from the cold, calculating way she looked him up and down that she was a whore. She saw only a man, a rutting beast, and smiled. She loosened her cloak and Sasportas glimpsed her red velvet gown trimmed in black showing just the faintest trace of the top of her white breasts with, dangling between them, a key on a gold chain. The girl looked around with undisguised curiosity.

—What is your name?

—Rabbi, my name is Sara.

—Where are you from?

—From the village of Poznitz in Poland.

She spoke poor Yiddish, mixed with the local Dutch dialect and Polish words.

—And where is your habitation in this city, my child?

She looked at him slyly and before answering she looked around the room again, at the lectern and the books, the writing paper and ink, and finally at the humble, hard cot where he slept. Her smile turned into a suggestive smirk and she stared at the bed before looking back at him.

—I am a servant to Isabelle de Castro on the Nieuwe Achtergracht. Or I was, before she threw me out on the street.

She laughed, brazenly. Sasportas was acquainted with de Castro, a good Jew, one of the parnasim, a leader of the community and a dealer in spices.

—Why did she dismiss you?

—Oh, she was jealous.

Watching her smile Sasportas remembered the Proverbs: 'Such is the way of the adulteress. She smiles and eats her fill and says she has done no wrong.' He had to restrain himself from a desire to hit her.

—Why do you not return to your father's house?

—My father is dead.

—Have you no other family?

—No. I and my brother were the only ones who survived when Chieminiski's men came to our village.

For a moment Sasportas felt a huge pair of black wings beating above the room, a monstrous shadow fell on his heart and under his kaftan he touched the amulet with the sacred words folded inside it.

Accursed be the name!

Sasportas had read the accounts of the events in Poland in the black year of 1648, and he had seen the woodcuts and prints made in this city. But worse was what he saw in the eyes of those who had come west to escape the Terror. Thousands of Jews, hundreds of thousands, some said, had died like animals. In every town that the Cossacks had taken, they had killed every man, woman and child. They had burnt the synagogues, committed unspeakable acts with the Torah, set fire to entire villages, drowned the Jews in the rivers, buried them alive, hacked them with their swords till their arms were weary and their swords blunt. Those fleeing could go no further than Amsterdam, and still they wanted to run.

He thought of the city outside going about its business as if nothing had happened; even the Jews had forgotten, they were drinking and eating among the gentiles, as if his black hand would never reach this far.

Sasportas looked at the girl with new interest; he looked into her porcelain blue eyes for a shadow, but could not find one.

—How did you escape, my child?

—Pan Rosewitz, a Polish noblemen, rescued me and my brother. He raised us as his own children, we spoke Polish and were baptised in the Catholic Church. He was a good man, without him we would have died. A fine handsome man he was, a great horseman.

The girl looked dreamy for a moment.

—He gave me my own white pony, I used to ride it in the woods. I was so happy there!

Sasportas was thinking that she was the strangest Jewess he had ever seen. Now she started to walk around the room, peering into corners.

—How did you come to Amsterdam?

Her mood changed and she stopped and stared at him.

—Rabbi, you are a holy man and a magician they say, so I know I can tell you my story and you will understand.

Sasportas nodded non-commitally.

—I was happy there. Then ... one night ...

She paused and Sasportas noticed that it was for dramatic effect. He felt that she had told this story many times before, to others, to herself. She took on the air of an actress, but a very convincing one.

—One night, I fell asleep as usual and had a dream.

She glanced up at Sasportas, interrupting herself, eagerly:

—They say, Rabbi, that you can read dreams, that it is all in your books there.

She gestured with curiosity and prurient interest at the volumes of kabbalah on his table.

Sasportas was amazed at her effrontery.

—These are things you should not speak of child! Even men cannot study kabbalah until they are thirty years old! And married!

She frowned as if amused and continued her story.

—In this dream a man appeared to me and said he was my true father. He had been killed by the Cossacks. My father lifted me up in his arms and we flew. He carried me through the air for many hundreds of miles. We passed over fields and mountains and rivers, and I saw all the villages below, with churches and synagogues, and forests. And then we came to a graveyard. My father told me that all my ancestors were buried here. He told me that they were all good Jews.

She leaned forward and whispered almost conspiratorially to Sasportas.

—And he told me many other things too, Rabbi.

She winked, looked around as if at unspecified spectators, and then continued.

—He carried me back to my bed, and when I woke I remembered it all. I realised who I was and what I must do. So I left the village and walked till I got here. My father told me to come here in the dream. I want to become a good Jewess, Rabbi. I am studying the holy tongue, and the Talmud, though they say it is not for girls.

Sasportas stood up, his anger rising.

—No, indeed! You should forget this nonsense about dreams. And why are you not married? You should be raising children and keeping the house. That is how you can be a good Jewess!

A thought suddenly struck Sasportas. She smirked as he scrutinised her carefully. Her figure, her face, her eyes. What if she were not a Jewess at all? What if her story was not true? But ... his mind ran down quickly through the possibilities. Why would a girl pretend to be a Jewess if she were not? Why would she leave her father's house and her native village and travel across Europe to here, to be a servant and to be a whore, if his suspicions were correct. Why would she choose to become an outcast, a refugee?

He could think of no answer. But her story was so preposterous, it was no wonder that the people had brought her here. The girl was clearly mad.

But now she answered him, in a different voice than before. This time she was serious, calm.

—Oh I will, Rabbi, I will. You see, in the dream my father told me ...

She leaned forward and told him, as if delivering good news:

—I will marry the Messiah!

Shrieks of horrified satisfaction erupted behind the door where Sasportas knew now the rabble had been waiting, listening. Furious, he grabbed his stick and started to hit the girl.

—Whore! Anathema! Get out of my sight!

She didn't move. His stick bit into her, the flesh of her arms and legs, he could feel the thwack against her thighs, the firm muscled flesh pressing back against his blows, but she didn't move. She just looked at him. The door had burst open and the Jews rushed in with hands in the air, horrified but also pleased that she had performed so well for the Rabbi, now he could see what she was like, what should we do with her?

He had no answer for them.

He hit her on the back and shoulders as she turned to go, cursing her.

—Harlot! Blasphemer! I expel you from the community! Let every Jewish door be closed to you!

The people gasped, they had not expected anything so harsh. Expulsion from the community was like a death sentence to them. But Sara seemed unmoved. She smiled.

—I've had enough of the cold here anyway. I have always dreamed of the South. Perhaps I will go to the Middle Sea ...

Slowly, still smiling, Sara walked out, and for an instant Sasportas had a vision of her buttocks shifting sinuously under her clothes. And that was the last he had ever seen of her.

He had hunted the rabble out of his room, and sat down, breathing heavily, his heart pounding.

Those words had branded themselves into his memory in letters of fire:

I will marry the messiah!

But it was only twenty years after, as he wrote his history, that he saw their other meaning, why she had smiled that way at him. What if she had meant something completely different, that the man she will marry would become the Messiah? No, he thought, it was not possible. It could not be that one woman's mad ambition had nearly brought about the end of the Jewish people?

But he could have imagined none of that, that night in Amsterdam, when, exhausted, Sasportas lay down his pen and stretched on his cot. Muttering prayers, half-dreading, half-eager for what his dreams would bring this night.

NESSA O'MAHONY

Those of us left   *for K.L.*

Three of us here,
four if you count the collie dog
you didn't meet though heard about
the last time we spoke;
you'd laughed
at my cosy domesticity,
compared notes on dust,
on box unpacking,
made plans for the weekend.

Those of us left
can't plan yet,
can barely put
one foot
in front of the other
though the pressure
on the leash,
an animal's hunger
for strange sights and smells,
reminds us that we must.

I grapple your lover's grief,
try to stifle the anger
that rises in waves.
It might help
if I knew who to target:
The you in that box?
Me?
The stone I kick
into the river?

MARY O'MALLEY

Palimpsest

I WALK UP FROM THE SEINE, from my overpriced café crème on the edge of the Isle St Lois, because it is Sunday, because I have renegued on a visit to someone I like – I go into Notre Dame, drawn by voices of great purity intoning a hymn to the Virgin at the ten o'clock mass,

I listen, and am steadied as I always am in this, my favourite Cathedral, intimate as a small town, or a village on the lower East side of New York.

I walk clockwise against the flow of the crowd – I never did get the flow of the crowd right – to the back, past the as-yet uncleaned 'Crown of Light' that will hang again over the central transept but now sits at head level separated by a simple low railing. I kneel in the Chaple of Rest at the back, the place I always kneel, or sit, and see that it is Christ's crown of thorns on a man like a movie star, in a print like a Dürer but softer, that I am worshipping. I am reminded of the words Bobby Kennedy quoted at his brother's funeral:

'... Wisdom by the awful grace of God,' not Christ, or Augustine nor yet Paul, bur Aeschylus.

And then I walk back, via Rue Mouffetard, to my cell in the Irish College.

What do I think when I think of home?

The hill, sweet as the curve of a whale, the cave under it, the Victorian folly, a gazebo, product of the madness of people who colonized us – the West was infested with Victorians having picnics in their bizarre teahouses on hills, islands, remote headlands, served by a retinue of native bearers, as if they were in India, as if the weather were tropical.

Beside the hill a lookout for use during the war, the castle on its flank, and always beside me my father, pointing out animal burrows and birds, showing the way.

But I was never allowed to go out at night and hold the torch when the men netted the river for eels, when I used to lift a corner of the thin bedroom curtain, careful not to wake the others and be found out. That was when I saw shadows and the occasional sign of village nightlife – I saw badgers shuffling, a fox flickering in the moonlight as she passed, the morse code of a plane stitching new stars across the mink pelt of the sky.

A fox, like a brooch on the collar of a woman crossing the bridge onto the Isle St Louis. And on the bridge, closed off to traffic, a clown moves through his slow routine, his tools around him; unicycle, paraffin, skittles and fire. He is young, supple, beautiful, and his face holds an easy friendliness and lacks armour. He moves into the crowd in this, the loveliest heart of the city, the full brass band assembling outside BHV, the cops on their all-important radios emptying the streets for the roller skaters, who stream like a river undammed along the Seine, across three bridges. One woman stands out. She is wearing a long red faux-fur coat, moving far off among the sea of browns, a flame through the Winter furze.

The present landscape is underscored with the maps and palimpsests of the past and, for us, the past is peopled, so the landscape, the twin towers of Slyne Head and the small road to Ballinlame, is the setting for what happened.

For people such as James, he being an outsider and considered odd, one hot day coming up to Granny's house to ask for water. Refused to come in for tea, just water Ma'am is all, leaving his wife at the end of the boreen, refusing even to step inside, then taking the mug of Spring water and pouring it over the roots of the bunch of flowers in his hand, so that they would survive and not die before they got home.

'I wouldn't mind,' Granny said, 'but they were weeds. Sure he could have picked weeds out of the drain at home.'

Such were our small entertainments. I can see those weeds now, a pinkish mauve flower on the thick stalks, and the water running over them and the scraped face of the man bending tenderly towards them, nursing them back to life as if they were the finest roses. In some alternative universe, according to quantum theory, he and Mary are still walking the road, bending towards one another in animated conversation, she looking as if she got the worst of it, following her husband to Silverhill.

LIAM Ó MUIRTHILE

Garsún

Garsún na súl úd
go raibh giorriacha
ag léimt ina cheann
amach as líonta lucht fiaigh,
go raibh breac abhann
go ciúin ann ina cheann
sa linn dubh fé chrann órga

is mise é.

Is eol duit nithe fé rún
a chréatúirín nach eol
d'aon duine beo
ach d'uisce agus don ngaoth,
is b'fhéidir don dobharchú
rúnmhar a thumann san abhainn
istoíche le heagla roimh an saol.

Is eol dom do ghortu beo
do chroi bocht leonta
inis anois dom e,
cuir do dhul fein air
eisteod go humhal leat
t'rom do laimhin
ragham ag siul le cheile

is tusa me.

Boy

boy with deep eyes
hares cavorting
in his skull
leaping from the hunters' nets,
a trout resting
quietly in his head –
black pool beneath a tree of gold

i am he

secretly, little creature,
you came to know those things
unknown to all
save for the water and the wind,
maybe the elusive otter knows all about it
diving into the river
at night in fear of the world

i know the hurt you live
your scarred heart
tell me now
in your own words
i'll listen humbly
give me your tiny hand
we'll walk together

i am you

(Translated by Gabriel Rosenstock)

MICHEAL O'SIADHAIL

Conversation with Goya

So knowing, Goya, as you turn and stare,
Pot-hatted matador still stabbing paint,
Your streetwise eye declaring 'I'm no saint,
I love this world with all its earthenware'.
You're carnal as the heavens you've portrayed
In frescoes painted on Antonio's dome;
No God here tipping Adam's hand in Rome,
Just people crowding round a balustrade.
Your cherubs caught in life's own push and shove
Gaze down at us below where now instead
Seductive angels pillar up the sky;
Your brush must never see beyond the eye:
Baroque's high heaven stood so on its head,
A world looks up and sees itself above.

When I look up I only see the sky –
Both hell and heaven lurk within the mind;
I want them both so turn my sceptic eye
And daub the plainer face of human kind.
For me no wispy classic lines redeem
The man, the rogue, the whore, the thief, the nark;
We're close to nature in our most extreme,
The blots and scribbles of our light and dark.
I've seen the greats but never can look back.
I want to show the cruel Spain I know,
Garrotte and war, the whole unholy show;
Though in the end such immanence turns black.
My ears are sealed, my head a padded cell,
I paint dark murals in my deaf man's shell.

Ambition got you there, your inner drive
And though you never chose to faun or shirk
Some artist's bullish instinct to survive
Just shrugs as if to say 'all work is work'.
O yes, a sharp enlightenment critique
But you're still painter to the royal court;
Despite your fiery independent streak
For forty years you live by their support.
A Bourbon leaves and worse then comes to worst –
But one king gone another reigns supreme –
You paint Napoleon's José the First,
You're ribboned portraitist to each regime.
For all your moral rage and posturing,
A trimmer who survives from king to king.

My witches and my scenes of sin or crime,
Caprichos with their pointed wit and dart,
All banderillas in the neck of time
Which shifts now towards a new Romantic art.
Though I am called the first great modernist,
A future movement's distant lightening rod;
My best is still compassion's unclenched fist,
The shining eye before the firing-squad.
Beyond the portraitist and royal hack
Or any darker world of deaf caprice
My testament to you the Third of May
Where fusiliers have turned their nameless back
And bend to execute their point-blank prey;
My lamp of pity lights the victim's face.

LEANNE O'SULLIVAN

A Healing

That first day of springtime thaw when the ice
began to melt and pour down the mountains,
I walked to the top of the old mining road
to hear all the slow loosening and letting go,
the kick-back of copper and clay from my heels,
the steady blasts following like the sound
of another person's footfall on the shale
spirited behind me; the streams that thundered
down to disappear again underground
so that the whole place was all tremble and go,
lightening into a stiller and clearer air.
I loved the copper-lit, the downhill skid and slack,
the water-roar out of time turning back
with so much sound and rush that it seemed
to be gathering strength from ore and dust and clay,
under the shade of that green and beaten ground.

MAEVE O'SULLIVAN

Sunday, Women Drying Their Hair

Bare-legged, in light, pale clothing,
three young women stand on an urban rooftop:
New York, probably, or some other big city.
They are letting the wind dry their hair
while white garments sway on a line behind them,
and the chimney beside them casts a long shadow.

It is 1912, and Sloan's subjects could be sisters:
one redhead in a green skirt, one brunette, one blonde.
The brunette looks approvingly at the redhead,
while the blonde brushes her hair hanging
like a curtain, her head tilted to the right,
the left hand on her hip for balance.

I imagine they are chatting about the night before;
what they did, who they saw dancing, girl talk.
One of them could be softly humming
'After the Ball' or something jazzy;
no World War to bother them yet, and no Depression,
this year forever marked by a ship called the Titanic.

This is how I would like *my* three sisters to be:
close, relaxed, hanging out happily,
the brunette smiling at the redhead, the blonde
still long-haired and carefree, and me,
the youngest girl, looking on
from the gallery, taking it all in.

PAUL PERRY

To the Book of Kells

He woke after what seemed
like a hundred years of sleep,
found his clothes, recently
returned to him, walked down

the stairs and out into the daylight.
He walked slowly. It felt
like he was walking on the moon.
He rose and wavered,

floated, sprang from one foot
to the other. Everything
sped by him. Cars, people,
and dreams. His own thoughts

remained deliberate, careful.
Past the brewery, down by the river
shining in sunlight, he walked.
When he reached the Book in its tower

he gazed at its arcane colours
and curlicues and heard the vellum
like wind through a field soughing
and shifting. He thought of the island

Iona and the visions of the monks and
then of his own recent and strange
imaginings. Fantastical paranoia.
IRA plots, accusations, kidnappings

and tortures. After swimming
in the sea of the Book, he shook
himself dry and walked slowly
along the river, dark now, but still

with hints of gold and green.
No one noticed when he returned
or that he had been gone
in the first place. He went to the bathroom,

removed his clothes, took his robe
and went back to bed. It was not
night, but he closed his eyes anyway
and entered not darkness but

another world where the Book began
to grow, gain strength, and as he fell
into a fitful sleep, to thread and stitch
its way tightly and colourfully into his dreams.

BILLY RAMSELL

What normal people do

What Frankie values most of all is conversation. He's got four tellies
in his gaff now, four radios, four mobiles that ring sometimes.

Frankie's no talker but he can listen for Ireland, man.
That's why he's so worked-up about the coffee-places,

about the silent screens, the private privacies,
that fill the cafés on French Church Street now.

All the banter Frankie loved is gone, gone, gone.
There's only whispered conversations now, or none.

And this silence puts the heart across our Frankie Fitz
and then Frank gets cross till he's bulling

at the sight of the blue suit well-fed with his ear-buds in
and frappuccino, the black man's baggy status update,

the auburn-haired thin one staring, as she chews cup-cake cud,
into her laptop's flickering well. Talk. Talk. Those dirty screens'
      dirty glow.

And he just grinds thigh-flesh against his tenuous pocket-lining,
till his nails slip through the polyester,

goes home and puts his tellies on at full blast all at once,
does this little shimmy on the landing, don't tell anyone that,

watches tissue after tissue melt and blacken in the fireplace.
Talk. Talk. Metal blue. Pink, red. The pavement's warm soupy gush.

Burnt brown. Spreading black. Talk, talk. Those dirty screens.
Oh you might even think old Frankie's harmless, even pitiful,

a faggot, a slapless fuck, their blank magnetic faces,
but you'd be about a hundred per cent wrong about that,

cos you're gonna know about this uncalled-for silent treatment,
this dissatisfaction will be advertised in no uncertain terms.

The paper flakes wither. The paper flakes convulse and char.
People will find out. People are gonna know.

MAURICE RIORDAN

Stars and Jasmine

Each of them has been a god many times:
cat, hedgehog and – our summer interloper – the tortoise.
A perfect triangle, they can neither eat
nor marry one another.
And tonight they are gods
under the jasmine under the stars.

Already the hedgehog has scoffed the cat's supper
and she's walked nonplussed beside him
escaping headlong into the bushes.
Wisely now, she keeps an eye on him there,
and on the tortoise
noisily criss-crossing the gravel.

For the cat, jasmine is white
but the stars have colours.
For the hedgehog, there are no stars
only a sky of jasmine,
against which he sniffs something dark,
outlined like a bird of prey.

Wisely, the tortoise ignores both jasmine and stars.
Isn't it enough, she says, to carry the sky on your back,
a sky that is solid, mathematical and delicately coloured –
on which someone, too, has painted
our neighbours' address: 9a Surrey Rd.
Come September, we will post her through their letterbox.

MARK ROPER

All Up

Water in the saltmarsh pools
trembling over footmarked mud
and hawthorn stooping under
sea-wind's thump and battery,
lapwing all lift-off and lapse
and freshening the race track
a shower of golden plover –
a side-on flash of cash, a sketch
of shimmery fish-scale –
chevrons of geese, creak
of their unoiled complaint,
the haunt-call of a curlew,
an oystercatcher's piping,
a single wigeon whistling
to and from another world
and even the stationary swans,
when a dog launches itself in
and doggypaddles towards them,
even the swans harness their carts,
haul the long improbable logs
of their bodies off the lake
and everything's up in the air
and all over the place save
for the cormorant caught
in monofilament, drowned,
and the moorhen in a channel
caught in monofilament, about
to drown, and by the time
we pass by again, drowned.

GABRIEL ROSENSTOCK

An extract from **Ólann mo Mhiúil as an nGainséis**

Ocean of Light ... Night is falling. We light the citrus candles which keep the insects away. We open a bottle of wine. In the water the shadows dance an ancient waltz and the music of nature reminds us that the darkness of night is just a temporary aberration and the world will soon bathe again in an ocean of light.

> an egret stands in a lagoon
> on the flagstones
> sound of washed clothes

I have a bad night on that barge – between the heat, mosquitoes and the incessant crowing of the cockerels – and there is another sound, a sound like rolling thunder. If it's not the sky rumbling, it must be the sound of *vedi vashipadu* – the ritual of explosions, a tradition which makes a bigger racket than thunder ever would.

A visit next morning to St Mary's Cathedral, the Syrian Catholic Cathedral of Cheripally. The dead are kept in the graveyard here for three or four years before their bones are transferred to the ossuary so that room can be made for the next batch of dead people. The bones in the ossuary are burnt each time it becomes full. The walls of the church are decorated with wall hangings made from plants. Characters from the Old Testament for the most part, Noah to the fore. One can understand how people who live and work on water would have a special empathy with the honest soul that was Noah.

Christianity has become over-Westernised, repulsively so in some of its fundamentalist forms. I think of Henri le Saux, the

Benedictine monk from Brittany, who ended up near the holy mountain of Arunachala in India and became Swami Abhishiktananda, whose central belief was as follows:

> 'Man's primary task is to penetrate within and there discover himself. Whoever has not found himself within himself has not yet found God; and whoever has not found God within himself has not yet found himself …'

QUACK-QUACK! There are boats out in the water here which are very similar to the Irish *naomhóg* or curragh. They are collecting shellfish. Once opened, the shells are used to make cement. A boat passes us, full of clay pots. And who's this bucko who's heading in our direction now? Duck salesman! chirps a member of the crew who hasn't spoken a word until now. No doubt about it, they're all out today. In the river there are men standing, up to their waists in water, washing themselves and shaving. On the canal bank, a group of boys relax quietly, their fishing rods tipping the surface of the water. If paradise exists, then it must be a water paradise rather than a paradise of air. The souls of the just eddying and flowing from place to place, rippling out into eternity. And there will be no mosquitoes allowed into this Heaven – not into the seventh heaven anyway.

Our driver is waiting for us. We've a bit of a journey ahead, uphill to the higher reaches of Kerala, an area that borders Tamil Nadu. This is the territory of the tiger – there is still the odd one left here, the occasional descendant of those few which weren't shot by the British during the era of the Raj. The driver of the car is a Christian, married to a Hindu. Neither family has spoken to one another for the past twenty years – and it doesn't look like they will anytime soon either. The guidebook for tourists claims that all religious groups in Kerala live in perfect harmony with one another; the reality is clearly a bit different, however. There are religious and ethnic tensions simmering beneath the surface although they are not half as obvious here as they are in other parts of India.

We've reached Thekaddy. I thought the place would be at too high an altitude, the air too cool – that it would be too far away from the waterways for the mosquitoes to live here. I was wrong! They're here too, those pesky little monsters. I wake during the night to spray more anti-mosquito repellent on myself and to put on a long-sleeved shirt. Eithne sprinkles lemongrass oil on the four corners of the bed, not unlike somebody blessing the bed with holy water in days of yore. Still, the mosquitoes keep coming. Our next resort is prayer. What saint would hear our plea? Listen here, didn't Saint Colm have a fly as his pet? Right so. Here we go.

A Naomh Colm Cille a raibh peata cuileoige agat
Cosain sinn, impímid ort, ar na diabhail bheaga go léir
Mo chreach is mo chás!
Atá ag teacht idir sinn agus codladh na hoíche.
Múin míneas dóibh agus béasa
Agus tabhair slán sinn as ucht Dé
Sinne agus gach neach eile atá i bpéin anocht in Thekaddy, Áiméan.

St. Columba, you who had a pet fly
Protect us we implore you from all wee devils
Oh woe and desolation!
That come between us and a night's sleep.
Teach them gentleness and manners
And bring us out of harm's way in the name of God
We and everyone else in pain tonight in Thekaddy, Amen.
It worked!

translated from the Irish by Micheál Ó hAodha

PETER SHERIDAN

Me to Play
(First Chapter of a Memoir)

1

I WAS HOOKED on theatre from the get go. I have my father to thank and blame for that. In April of 1967 our family was torn apart when Frankie, my ten-year-old brother, died of a brain tumour. No one took it harder than Da. He went from being a man who never missed work, to a man who never went to work. He started to suffer severe migraine and spent most of his days in bed with a damp facecloth on his forehead. The shutters were permanently closed and we tiptoed around the house so as not to wake him. He blamed himself for the genetic flaw that had killed Frankie and he waited for it to take him, too. He wanted to die. I know that because I wanted to die also. There had been an incident, I'd told no one about it, when Frankie had banged his head off the road out scutting on the back of a horse and cart with me. I went to sleep every night with the image of his bruised face in my head. I wanted to tell my father that it wasn't genetic, but the decision was taken from me. He got out of bed, came down to the kitchen and told Ma that the migraine was gone.

'That's great, Da,' she said, 'you'll be going back to work, so.'

'No, I won't be going to work. I'm going to start a drama group. I've always wanted to get up on a stage and act out a part.'

'Do you mean act out a part like Gary Cooper in *High Noon*?'

'Yes, just like Gary Cooper in *High Noon*.'

It was his favourite film. He brought Ma to see it for their wedding anniversary and when he came home he acted it out for us in the kitchen, on the stairs and out in the back yard staring in the window, frightening us to death in a nice way. He had other stories, too, like *The Old Man and the Sea,* and one about a time he tried to sell ice-cream off a bike on Dollymount Strand only to discover that his stock had melted. He had sagas about Cuchulainn and Ferdia and another about his father, Grandad Jim, who fought with the IRA in 1916 against the British and ended up escaping from a gaol in Wales after a key was brought in hidden in a Christmas cake. They were good stories but not as good as *High Noon.* When Da did Gary Cooper you could hear the clock ticking, marking out the tension, making you scared out of your wits. Ma had to keep a straight face but sometimes you could see the hint of a smile, especially when Da sang 'Do Not Forsake me, oh my Darling.' I never heard my father tell my mother that he loved her, but when Da acted out being Gary Cooper that was as close as he came.

The drama group saved our family. Da became an actor because the only other option for him was to give up and die. He decided to fulfill his lifelong ambition and he never would have done it if Frankie had lived. It took Frankie's death for him to realise the importance of embracing his dreams. He asked us all to gather in the Oriel Hall for a play reading. I went out of curiosity. I'd never seen a play acted out, apart from a pantomime. We read plays in school and learned speeches off by heart to regurgitate at exam time, a process that made drama about as exciting as a funeral. We sat around a table in the Oriel Hall and read plays by Sean O'Casey, WB Yeats, John Millington Synge, Hugh Leonard and Brendan Behan.

It was an intimate experience because we shared scripts and, even though Da had been brought back to life, his redemption did nothing for his profligacy – it was four copies between twenty people. We decided on *Shadow of a Gunman* for our first outing and I was offered the part of Tommie Owens which I duly accepted. I wrote out my part in a copybook so that I could learn the lines (mercifully he only appears in the first act of the play). It was fascinating to read it back in my own handwriting, somehow it made the character feel more personal. When I started writing my own plays some years later, I kept up the practice of doing it by longhand because it felt more connected, more real, and brought me back to where my journey in theatre began.

Da called the drama group the 'Saint Laurence O'Toole's Musical and Dramatic Society', after the parish where we all lived. There was no discussion regarding the name. Da designed a rubber stamp and sent me to collect it from a shop in Capel Street. We spent one whole rehearsal with the stamp, an ink pad and squares of cardboard making out tickets for the first performance of *The Shadow of a Gunman*. A space had been left at the bottom for the date, the time and the price of admission which, after much argument, was left at 2/6d. for the evening show and 1/6d. for the Saturday matinee.

I hated the name. It sounded like we were a church group that put on passion plays at Easter, or performed little dramas as part of the mass. It had a craw-thumper feel to it which was starkly at odds with the message of the play. O'Casey himself had been born a Protestant but had rejected religion at an early age in favour of socialism. He had lived in a two-storey house at number 18 Abercorn Road – our family had lived in a cottage at number 12 until a growing brood forced the move (in 1956 when I was four) to a bigger house in Seville Place – and it was while he lived there that O'Casey first turned his hand to writing. In 1915, with an inheritance left to him by his mother, he self-published a history of the Irish Citizen Army under the pseudonym, P O'Cathasaigh.

I expressed my reservations on the name to my brother Shea. He hated it, too.

'I'll tell him we don't like it,' Shea said. 'There's no point in bottling it up.'

'No, don't say anything. I'll bring it up with him. There's less chance of a row that way,' I said.

I had a better relationship with him than Shea. They rubbed each other up the wrong way most of the time. Shea had an uncanny ability to get under his skin. It was a primitive, Oedipal thing. Ma adored Shea and never hid her adoration. I'm sure Da must have felt displaced in the competition for Ma's affections. Shea, for his part, exulted in and exploited his position at every opportunity.

'Who do you love the most, Ma?' he would say when the Sunday jelly and ice-cream was being doled out. Ma would tut at him through a smile and Shea would glory in the apotheosis that ensured his portion would be larger than everyone else's.

I decided to raise the question with Da on the final Saturday night of the run in the Oriel Hall. The show had gone brilliantly. Six sold-out performances. Da at the top of his game, bringing down the house in his role as the pedlar, Seumas Shields. He made an emotional curtain speech, thanking everyone who'd attended and, in a veiled reference to Frankie, he acknowledged those who couldn't be there. He singled out Father Freaney, or to be accurate, the 'Reverend Father,' for gracing the play with his presence. From my position on the stage, I caught Shea throwing his eyes to heaven – he was standing in directorial mode at the back – and while I couldn't mirror his revulsion, I felt it.

Later that night, sitting around the table in Seville Place, we were back to something like a proper family again. Da was polishing off a bottle of stout, Ma was cutting a loaf to make the supper and I was a little tipsy. I picked my moment and let my words slide across to Da, direct and uninhibited.

'There's going to be trouble over the name of the group,' I said.

There was no immediate reaction. His brow furrowed and he locked on me with concerned eyes.

'You're slurring your words,' he said.

Yes, I was slurring my words, he was right. I was celebrating. Like everyone else in the Saint Laurence O'Toole's Musical and Dramatic Society. We'd come to the end of a successful run, our first outing in front of the public and I was entitled to be a little drunk. I'd spent three months inside the skin of Tommie Owens, a little twirp of an alcoholic, and just as he was entitled to his opinion on the state of the world, I was entitled to an opinion on the state of our lousy name.

'You shouldn't be drinking,' Ma said, 'you're only sixteen years of age.'

'I'm nearly seventeen,' I said.

'You're drunk, that's what you are,' she said.

'I'm not drunk, I'm tipsy.'

'You should steer clear of alcohol if you can't control it,' Da said. 'It will bite you on the arse before you know it.'

'Alcohol's my friend, that's all I'm going to say.'

It was, too. My dependable, foolproof, one hundred per cent friend. I didn't know of its power until I was introduced to it at Frankie's wake. Cuz, a man with a purple nose who was related to my father, poured me a whiskey, added a drop of peppermint to it and told me that it would ease the pain. He told me that Jameson was the working man's friend. It burned me on the insides going down but a few minutes later I was filled with a warm glow. I managed to pour a second Jemmy and pep down my throat. The movie of Frankie falling off the horse and cart disappeared from my brain and I slept that night like a baby. It was a sleep without guilt. I woke up that morning, the day of his funeral and forgot that he was dead. It was such a shock when I remembered that he was in his coffin.

'You took the pledge at your confirmation, in case you've forgotten,' Ma said.

'I don't forget things,' I said.

'You were supposed to abstain until you were eighteen,' Da said.

'I remember. I know what I promised.'

'You can take it again,' Ma said. 'You can pledge yourself in front of Father Freaney. He'd see you in the sacristy before devotions.'

It was the perfect opportunity to go on the attack. There were

lines in *The Shadow of a Gunman* castigating the church for
enslaving the people of Ireland. They were more than lines, they
were speeches and Da's character, Seumas Shields, had many of
them. I was going to trot them out to Ma and put her in her place.
I knew that my mouth could not keep up with my brain, however.
I knew I would start slurring and I couldn't give them that
opportunity again. I wanted to stick with the argument in hand.
The name of the group was too religious, too Catholic, too
subservient. Especially for a group dedicated to O'Casey, a
Protestant writer who'd left Ireland and become a communist.
Something had to be done and I was determined to carry the fight.
I decided to empty my bladder before I went over the top.

I sat on the toilet bowl with my head in my hands and thought
about Da. He wasn't an overtly religious man but maybe he had
made a pact with God. I once caught him on his hands and knees
up on the roof, invoking the holy name.

'Jesus, if you are who you are, come to my aid ...'

We were repairing slates and I'd gone down to get some
flashing. I came back up and there he was, talking to himself. I
said nothing, I just watched. There was a quiver in his voice. I
stayed at the top of the ladder, observing him. He became
conscious of me and stopped, searching on the ground for nails or
something, before he took the flashing off me and started to cut it
with a rusty old scissors.

'Never be afraid to get on your knees and ask God for help,'
he said. 'It takes a man to do that.'

It was the only advice he ever gave me about religion. I don't
know what he was praying for. Maybe he was praying for the third
one in a treble to come in. Or, more likely, he'd lost the
housekeeping money on a 'good thing' and hadn't yet told Ma.
Maybe he was thanking God for having taken away his migraine.
Maybe he had made a pact over the name of the drama group and
couldn't go back on his word. Everything came back to Frankie,
that's how it was in our family. The mere mention of his name was
enough to open the wound and make it bleed.

I came back from the bathroom and dived straight into a crusty slice of turnover smothered in bread and jam. I knew they'd been talking about me, the way you do. Da finished off his bottle of stout and Ma buttered more bread. I cracked into the crust and washed it down with perfectly brewed tea. Ma kept the family together, she had that gift, of not falling apart. Thanks to her, Da was back in the fold. I was acting on the stage with him but it hadn't brought us together. It appeared close and connected because of the emotional engagement between the characters on stage. I could hold his hand (and did) during the final bow, I could put my arm around his shoulder but offstage any kind of physical contact seemed impossible. I needed him. I needed his strength and his forgiveness. I needed to tell him about my awful dreams, I needed to tell him and I needed him to make it all right for me, the way he'd always done since I was a child. I couldn't go there with him. He wasn't available to me. The only escape I had was Jameson.

Da finished his bottle of stout and turned to the matter in hand. He wanted to know what faction in the drama group didn't like the name.

'It's not a faction,' I said. 'There are no factions.'

'There are always factions, that's how life works,' he said.

'I'm not in a faction.'

'Maybe you should be. Maybe it would do you good.'

'I'm not into politics, I hate that stuff.'

'If you were in the right faction you might be the next king of the castle.'

'What are you talking about?'

'I don't know, I'm not planning a coup, am I?'

It was Da at his worst, deliberately trying to rise a row. My brain couldn't keep up with him. After a half an hour or so, I declared myself a faction and went to bed.

⤴

Da always strove to unite the community of Saint Laurence O'Toole's, a parish divided along social and economic lines. On one side were the professional classes that lived in the houses around Seville Place, Emerald Street and Oriel Street; on the other were the dockers and manual labourers that lived in the Corporation flats. There were two tribes, divided by Sheriff Street, and they didn't mix much, if at all. They drank in different pubs and knelt on opposite sides in the church at Sunday mass. Da never subscribed to this idea and from an early age he insisted that we play with the children from the flats in their playground in Sheriff Street. We were the only family from our side to do so.

Tina Molloy was the only member of the drama group from the flats. She was one of fourteen children and, being the eldest, she left primary school at thirteen and went straight to work in Manning's cake shop on Parnell Street. She was extrememly bright and intelligent and the best actor in the company. She played Minnie Powell in *The Shadow of a Gunman,* her own life of struggle embodying much of the O'Casey heroine. In the course of rehearsing and performing the play, I fell in love with her.

Tina had a very gentle nature and although her flat in Brigid's Gardens was a hive of mad, raucous activity, she never raised her voice but was always heard. She had a deep faith and was a member of the Legion of Mary, an organisation I joined because I thought it might impress her. I didn't know at the time that the boys and girls met in separate rooms. Joining the Legion was the first of many wrong moves I was to make where Tina was concerned. I befriended her younger brother, Larry, and tried to talk him into joining the Legion of Mary, too.

'I might join the French Foreign Legion, go on a real adventure.'

'Your sister's in the Legion of Mary,' I scolded him. 'You trust Tina, don't you?'

'She's a holy Joe, she'll turn into a statue some day.'

I convinced Tina to make up a foursome on a day out to the

seaside at Bray. My friend Tommo Hogan and a girl he was chasing, Anna Hederman, were the other couple. We set off one Sunday on an early morning train. On arrival in Bray, we headed straight for the ghost train. Tommo and Anna sat in the front and immediately started kissing. I didn't know what to do. In the darkness that enveloped us, I put my arm around Tina. I turned to kiss her but I missed her face and my mouth ended up in her hair.

After our day out in Bray, I walked Tina home as far as the convent. There was a porchway, near to where the Legion of Mary meetings were held. I stopped at it.

'Thanks for a lovely day, Peter,' Tina said.

'I'm glad you enjoyed it.'

I could see that she meant it. She was such a truthful girl. So innocent and wide eyed. Yet, she was a woman. It wasn't an age thing. It had to do with her family and the fact that she supported them. She stood in Manning's cake shop ever day, not out of choice, but out of necessity.

'Would you like to kiss me?' Tina said.

I tried to think of something clever but all that came out was one word.

'Yes,' I said.

She turned her head to the side and moved towards me. I stepped in to meet her. Our lips touched. Hers were wet which was a lovely surprise. I kissed her for as long as I could and then she pulled back. I put my hand to her head and pulled her towards me. I put my lips against hers again. I tried to push my tongue into her mouth but she desisted.

'No tongues,' she said. 'Lips only.'

That porchway became our kissing place. I rehearsed with her in the Oriel Hall and afterwards went for chips with all the others to the chipper at the Five Lamps. Then I walked with her down Seville Place, and ostensibly left her home to the flats, only I never reached there, we stopped off at our porchway and kissed, lips only.

I never felt her tongue because that was the rule and I learned to keep it.

$$\Longleftrightarrow$$

Tina was inspired casting as Juno Boyle, the heroine of O'Casey's *Juno and the Paycock,* the author's follow up to *The Shadow of a Gunman,* and our second big production. She brought an authority and a maturity way beyond her years to it. My father played the Captain, her no-good husband, and it was fascinating for me to watch her in rehearsal contol him, just as she controlled me in my pursuit of her. She had a clear, delineated world view and she was not going to let any man steer her off course. In the story of the play, she falls for the false promise of the will and the riches it is going to bring, just as the Irish people had fallen for the promises of the newly formed Irish Free State. All we had done, in O'Casey's world view, was to replace one form of false hope with another. We were still enslaved. Juno becomes the potential for a new order when she rejects the old nationalism and cries out against the muderers of her beloved son, Johnny (played by Shea).

Where were you when me darlin' son was riddled with bullets. God, take away our hearts of stone and give us hearts of flesh. Take away this murderin' hate and give us Thine own eternal love.

I was sixteen when my father cast me as Joxer Daly in *Juno,* too young for the part by twenty-five years at least. O'Casey in his stage directions describes Joxer as a 'shoulder-shrugger' and there were plenty of those to be seen around Sheriff Street. I took Ostler Moore as my prototype, a small man with a connection to horses. He ambled more than walked. It was three steps forward and two back, with a little flick of his coat thrown in every now and then. He wore a permanent smile that was unaffected by the seasons or his mood. He spoke through it and sang through it whether the message was one of catastrophe or joy.

I put his physical quirks onto the character and tried them out in rehearsal. People were impressed. But there was still the problem of my age. I sat in front of the mirror, hating myself because I looked sixteen. I thought that if I gave myself a high forehead, it might help me become Joxer. So I started to cut my hair. The more I cut, the better it looked. By the time I finished, I had nothing left on top. Ma screamed when she saw me. I was delighted. I looked twenty years older. I didn't look like my father's son. I looked like his buddy.

Tina let me know that Ostler was coming to the play. It was our last night in the Oriel Hall. I had built my character on him and now I was about to parade it in front of him. In some of my quieter moments on stage, I observed him in the audience. He was sitting in the middle of the second row, impossible to tell if he was enjoying himself or in pain. In the play's infamous party scene, I closed my eyes and bawled out my 'shut-eyed' song, *She is Far From the Land.* I could hear his laugh wheezing back at me, and the rest of the audience joining in, not at my antics, but at his.

After the show, he hung out at the back of the hall. In the end, I found myself two feet from him, staring at the smile.

'You were gas, Joxer, I nearly broke me bollix laughing at you.'

'That's great,' I said.

'Your baldy head and all, bleedin' gas. You should come with a warning, do you know that?'

'Yeah, I know.'

'You forgot your words and all, that did it for me, I couldn't stop laughing, did serious damage to me bollix, I'm not joking you.'

'I'm glad you enjoyed it.'

'You remind me of someone. You do, no messin'. Know who you remind me of?'

I shook my head.

'The walk of you and all,' Ostler said. 'The bleedin' shoulders, you were very bleedin' funny, you were now, straight up. You had me in stitches.'

'That's great,' I said, not knowing what to say.

'Know who the funny walk reminded me of?'

'Not really.'

'Larry bleedin' Molloy. Tina's brother. You have him down to a tee. Bleedin' gas, I'm not codding you, you had me in stitches, Joxer.'

From that moment on, Ostler only ever called me Joxer. He invited me back to the Ball Alley pub in Sheriff Street because he wanted all his friends to meet me. He wanted to introduce Joxer to the community because he was a gas man, a man who could make people laugh. I was about to decline the invitation when it transpired that all the cast were going back to the Ball Alley for a last-night drink. So I ended up playing Joxer and performing some of the lines from the play and the shut-eyed song from the party scene.

By the time Ostler started singing 'Crazy' for the fourth time, shut-eyed to boot, Tina and I left the Ball Alley and headed down Sheriff Street. It was the perfect opportunity to walk her into St. Brigid's Gardens and maybe even have a cup of tea in her flat. It was her chance to introduce me to her parents, the way you would if you were comfortable, if you were genuine boyfriend material. As we walked along Sherrif Street towards the flats, Tina turned the corner and headed for the kissing porch.

It was sinful and dark. Our moment was interrupted by approaching voices. They were loud and aggressive, shouting across one another into the night sky. I broke off from the kiss and turned to see who it was. There was Skinnyah Geoghegan slugging from a bottle of whiskey. Then I saw Hardhead Wallace and Dommo Rowe, a few steps behind him. I turned back to Helena and put my arms around her neck.

'I think you should go home, Peter,' she whispered in my ear. 'I don't trust them.'

'They're just having a bit of a mess, that's all.'

'They're drunk. Go home now before they catch us.'

Her fear unsettled me. I knew that she wasn't afraid for herself.

It was me she was worried for. Why was I in danger? Was there something she wasn't telling me?

'Do you want me to walk you into the flats?' I said.

'No, I want you to go home. Now. Just get out of here. Trust me. They're up to no good.'

We stepped out of the porch, Tina turned right for the flats and I turned left for Seville Place. As she walked away from me, I heard her make conversation with Skinnyah and the others.

'Were you with him?' I heard Skinnyah ask.

'What were you doing with him?' Hardhead wanted to know. 'Did he put a hand on you?'

Tina said something but I couldn't make out what it was. Then Skinnyah roared out at the top of his voice.

'Stay away from our women, Shero, do you hear me?'

I decided to ignore him. I walked on purposefully, praying that my strategy of non-engagement was the right one.

I heard a bottle smash, followed by the sound of running feet. I broke into a fast walk as I headed around the corner into Seville Place. I put my hand in my pocket to get out the key and realised I hadn't got one. I had no idea who was at home, if anyone, and whether they were having supper or in bed. I'd loaned my key to Shea, I remembered. I'd last seen him in the Ball Alley. I wondered was he still there. I ran up the steps of our house and knocked on the door. I pressed the bell but didn't know if it rang or not. I knocked again on the door. I looked down the street to see Skinnyah, bottle in hand, coming after me. The front door opened. It was Shea. I fell in the door, just as Skinnyah got to the garden railings behind me. Shea slammed the door and we heard the stump of the bottle hit the wall, smack between the two large windows.

'Leave our women alone,' Skinnyah roared out before the other two joined in the baying chorus chorus.

Skinnyah came around to the house and knocked on the front door. The remains of the bottle he'd thrown was in the front garden. It glistened in the sun and caught my eye. I looked up and there in the distance was Tina's brother, Larry, sitting on the steps of the presbytery, keeping a distant watch.

'I'm sorry, Shero,' Skinnyah said, 'that was the drink talking last night.'

'That's all right, Skinnyah, I understand.'

'Keep your hands off our women and you'll be all right, ok!'

'I don't know what you mean?'

'Dick Elliot asked her out. She's one of us, do you understand?'

'Do you mean she's from the flats and she can't go out with me?'

'That's right. You're posh, so get yourself a posh bird to go out with.'

'I'll go out with Tina if that's what Tina wants.'

'Tina wants Dick. You can ask Larry if you don't believe me.'

Skinnyah turned and waved at Larry, who waved back. I knew I'd lost her. Dick and I had been close once. We both boxed for the British Railways club. So did his younger brother, Christy, who was always paired with me. We fought three times in the National Stadium and each time it was a draw. We were only kids and the crowd got a great laugh out of us because we stood in the middle of the ring, closed our eyes and threw punches at a hundred miles an hour. Christy went on to win a European title and fight professionally in America.

At age twelve, Dick befriended me. He was fifteen at the time. My parents were dead-set against it and I could never figure out why. Dick introduced me to the business of 'carrying cases'. We stood at the bottom of the steps at Amiens Street Station and when we spied someone in trouble with their luggage, we pounced. The trick was to get the case into your hand and start walking. Once they felt the relief of not having to lug all that weight, they'd never take the case back. Most of the time they were heading up to the Gresham Hotel in O'Connell Street or a bed and breakfast in Gardiner Street. The most we ever got was a pound for carrying two cases to Grooms in Parnell Square. We went down to a sweet shop in Guild Street with the money and bought two hundred and forty penny bars. They were toffee bars, rock hard, wrapped in silver paper that was nearly impossible to get off. I brought the bars home and my parents were disgusted. They thought it was a terrible waste of ten shillings. They couldn't understand why I didn't buy twelve bars and put nine shillings in my post office savings account.

I always thought they took a turn against Dick Elliot over the caramel bars. I now realise that it had nothing to do with that. They were embarrassed, or at least Da was, that Dick and I were working right outside his place of employment. What would his office colleagues say if they saw me? There were porters paid to help people with their luggage and here was his son and a gurrier stealing the work out from under their noses. Any time that Dick called for me at the house, they gave him the cold shoulder, Ma in particular. I once heard her asking him why he couldn't get a friend his own age to play with.

It was time for Dick's revenge. He was working on the docks as a tea boy, he had money and prospects. He could take Tina out of Manning's and make her comfortable. I couldn't fight for Tina because I knew in my heart that she didn't want me. She liked me and I liked her but she had made all these rules because she didn't have the heart to tell me to back off.

Skinnyah was the messenger. He'd come to tell me to stay on my side of the parish. Since I was a child, I'd broken that rule. I'd done it with Da's encouragement because that was his philosophy on life. The creation of the Saint Laurence O'Toole's Musical and Dramatic Society was an attempt to build bridges. It was driven by a belief that the theatre was not the preserve of one particular class and that talent was everywhere waiting to be discovered. For that reason, I wanted Tina to stay on in the group, even though I had lost her as a girlfriend.

GERARD SMYTH

Odd Man Out

In memory of K.R.

Among the gang of us you were the odd man out,
a believer in lucky charms,
a rabbit's foot gripped in your trembling hands,
the midge-bites on your arms like a personal stigmata.

Always the odd man out and always losing balance
after the first few sips from your glass of ale.
On the jukebox in Mario's Café you liked to play
Procol Harum: *A Whiter Shade of Pale.*

I saw you: all nerves, your face reddened,
twitching in the presence of girls from The Loreto;
saw you with your eyes to heaven
and saw you running like the devil when trouble came.

PETER SIRR

Delirium

Here drifts and falls, settles like snow
on the sill outside, and the floors of *now*
keep shifting from one absolute place
to another. It's as if
a hand has nudged her mind
from room to room through
a cloudy neighbourhood. Whose
furious life is this? She knits
her bones of memory and dream,
tumbles words like cards
in a changing game.
Everything falls down
and builds again, every sentence
is a machine for travelling.
We follow her now
to an apartment at the edge of the city
from which there is no return.
A forest grows round it, then a divorce
and now the place is full of duties
to be performed with difficulty,
food to be made for endless visitors
who will not help. Have you seen
what they've done to the attic?
She'll take us there, it's somewhere
between the ward and the end of the corridor,
though the stairs have vanished.
Who could have taken them?
Up there they are misapplying paint
and someone keeps moving the walls.
That's it, suddenly she says, looking hard
at us, someone keeps moving the walls.

RICHARD TILLINGHAST

Two Blues

Two blues – one called serenity,
one looks like the gathering storm.
I had a tube of each in my paint box in art school.
Colours spoke then.

Two blues,
the bland and the profound.
The ho-hum of a sky over Southern California –
you could call it *bleu celeste* or Egyptian blue.
Canaletto ground it out of lapis lazuli
for his Venetian skies.

That other blue might
have painted the scary ocean depths
off the Cape of Storms,
the colour of the sea in Winslow Homer's 'Gulf Stream,'
terror in the black castaway's eyes
almost blanked out with titanium white –

perhaps the same pigment
Homer daubed on as turbulence
atop the cobalt blue waves
running battleship grey through the comfortless Gulf Stream.
Sharks circle, knowing they will eat red meat
when night falls.

Those two colours tutor us in disaster,
at first as we have no hint of anything gone amiss,
anything to threaten our obliviousness,

our sense that life sparkles,
that there is such a thing as a career,
goals to be set and achieved.
Sometimes existence becomes a substance so depleted
one says to oneself:
If I can just make it across while the green walking light
stays illuminated,
then I'll walk halfway down the block
one step at a time,
watch the footing,
then back to the apartment,
make tea and, grasping the tray firmly with both hands,
inch back upstairs.

Though surely existence is limitless –
the spirit's measureless reach,
all the mind does,
memory's scope and inside-outness.
All that one understands now
which one previously had not.

To look out at traffic,
hear a taxi honk its horn,
and not have to venture out into otherness.

Recovering from an accident where one is obliged to
get both feet onto a step before moving
down to the next,
how enlivening it is on such a morning
to sit by the radiator and read sentences like these:

> *Drake had him beheaded alongside the gibbet from which*
> *Magellan hung his mutineers, Quesada and Mendoza,*
> *fifty-eight winters before. Wood preserves well in Patagonia.*

The coopers of the Pelican sawed the post and made tankards as souvenirs for the crew.

Two blues open the world.
I'm almost glad I fell.
How else would I be made aware
of those realities the staff in the emergency room
see nightly
and gladly try to hide
behind their talk of weekends
and Valentine's Day?

And these bruises on my face –
purple of the two black eyes
rainbowing to the mood indigo Duke Ellington wrote about.
Next an unsavory yellow
like the rind of a gone-off Persian melon
scattered among coffee grounds and empty *raki* bottles
outside a waterside restaurant in Istanbul
on the last day of August.

Burgundy blooms under my eyes
like the velvet of a sultan's caftan,
and then they glow with that
red in the morning
where sailors take warning.

COLM TÓIBÍN

Lodovick Bryskett

Two cotmen have come up the Slaney towards you.
They do not speak. They do not even see
You, as you scratch words on paper, conjuring up
An image of triumph with the sound of hooves
And banners flying against treachery.
The Slaney is glassy and treacherous.

There will be hopes always for fame and wealth
Versus the savage joy of being left alone
Near the turn of a river in a nearby country,
Half abandoned, half longed for, and much missed
Now that time has passed. You are locked
Into a game of failed and dismal glory.

You cross out the day's work, leaving no words
Unturned. The world is itself, has no need
Of you. The triumphant will is a rider-
Less horse, a dog barking in the night,
The dative case of a foreign language,
The moving clouds across an alien sky.

Life repeats. Night follows night; shadows
Seek further shadows; wood burns to ash;
More wood is cut. But the body weakens.
It is mostly sourness, endless until it ends.
The taste of something or a smell half known
Snarls at memory, a time long gone.

Turning towards the house in idleness
In the ruins of winter, you see a mist
Lingering in the hollow of the stone
Of the broken old monastery, and some-
Thing occurs to you then, like a fresh taste
Or an unfamiliar smell. This is

How change comes; it strikes you for no reason.
Will you now dream of sweet conquest, and then
Trumpets and the blaze of welcome, the heart
And the strong, fierce gut throbbing with grim need?
Or might this do instead, whiteness against
Stone, wispy, hardly worth the heeding?

EAMONN WALL

Waking, Softly, Tennessee

How our soft themes attach themselves
to rivers, flood plains, deciduous brown
golding, bright autumnal sun buffed up.
Entering Tennessee again the heart tung-
able of breath step, tray of artichoke set
in a beige order, the red of wine stretched
out beyond to low brown hills where
a gathering held noon time's reins
offering praise, each child dabbing a patch
of colour to a fine-lined page. We ramble
along by an old river, old Mississippi,
her movement of herself no grand gesture
of narration but a dreamless, awkward,
majestic sleep somnambulation. By car
or climbing route to air from Memphis,
we might note, though cannot note, how
cold the kestrel's pointed, indigent recall.

GRACE WELLS

A Cure for November

each thread a metaphor for a word in a sentence
or for a relationship
   — Alice Kettle

First gather coloured silks. Find those that bear
the names of flowers, violet, lilac, lavender,
take the hues of precious stones, turquoise, amber, jade.

Find tangerine, apricot, a dazzling lime.
Work in eggshell blue. Put the red from a robin's breast
beside gold so it lights like a fire in the hearth.

Take from the shelves a dictionary of stitches,
relearn the old tailoring, use God's eye stitch,
French knots, a plain herringbone.

Look about your house for loose objects,
beads, ribbon, a twist of string,
on a scrap of paper write the words *faith* and *courage*,

pin them all to the folds of this cloth. *Each thread*
a metaphor for a word in a sentence or a relationship,
sew out the contents your mind.

Trust when the needle plunges beneath fabric
to move unseen
the way laylines run below Avebury Henge.

Take cobalt blue and let your steady breath
illuminate, just as stained glass lights
on Remembrance Sunday when a lone bugler

plays 'The Last Post' in notes poppy red.
Add rain on the window, the way it falls
without fear or longing. Accept the accident

when you prick your finger and suddenly
there is a living drop of blood that you wipe
in the mouth the way women have done forever.

Take silver thread and wool soft as summer cloud,
place them in dialogue, let them speak out all
you have not found the strength to say.

Put in embarrassment, peppermint green envy,
white of shock and jaundiced yellow for your dull days,
darn them here beside your worst faults.

Unpick regret. In India it is the Festival of Light
they are setting small candles onto the Holy river,
cease your despair, employ a deep, personal witchcraft,

as you sew your life back together back together
                                        stitch by stitch.

DAVID WHEATLEY

Here's Looking at You

after Henri Michaux

Those who see me coming.
Me too, I'm onto them.
One day the cold will speak.
The cold will push the door open on Nothing.
And then, my hearties? What then?
Backsides to the wind, still swaggering,
bloated with others' voices and the lungs of the age,
I see the whole pack of you under one cover.
Hard at work? The palm tree shakes its arms.

And you combatants, soldiers of good heart, sold and unpaid.
Your glorious cause is beneath you. It'll be cold
in history's corridors.
How cold it is!
I see you be-aproned, and oh what a sight!
I see Christ too, and why not?
As he was two millennia back.
His beauty fading already.
His face gnawed by the kisses of Christians to come.
So are we still on for selling those seats in heaven?
I'm off then all, goodbye, my foot's on the escalator already.
Slán!

MACDARA WOODS

Song

Air: Dicey Reilly, slowly

Rose from my bed to mend my head
And fumbled out the door
Into the street to find relief
As many times before
With one sleeve on and one shoe off
Astray in time direction lost
And the start of my ruin was rising early

Still searching for the Angel
I went walking through despair
And when we met she told me
That I lived in disrepair
It's clear said she you're sorely pressed
Out here again and half undressed
Oh the start of my ruin was rising early

I thought that life was love revealed
That everyone agreed
That no one there intended harm
Kind lilies of the field
Beneath my feet no stones of doubt
Until the tide of youth went out
When the start of my ruin was rising early

I learned the cost of what I'd lost
But learning comes too late
So little time for love or rhyme
With the Piper at the Gate

To wreak in full the banishment
Of all who don't put by the rent
And the start of my ruin was rising early

And thus the years have come undone
To leave me walking still
Along the docks and promenades
In the morning river chill
There's no going back I must go on
Each night and day pass through the dawn
For the start of my ruin was rising early

VINCENT WOODS

Madness

Rose Wynne went mad
One summer's morning,
Stripped off her clothes,
Right down to her skin,
Ran down the lane
From the house, ran
Right across the road
In front of the crowd
Walking to mass.
Some of them said
She was laughing
Like a wild creature,
Some said she was crying
And screaming about a man,
A man, a man,
She ran straight out
In front of them
And down towards
The old Nunnery.
Her father and uncle
Went off after her,
And that was that.

McPadden's hackney
Came around three,
Took her away
To the Asylum in Sligo.

Mary would always remember
The shrug of the father's shoulders,
The way he raised his hat to all
And said 'Don't mind her now,
Don't mind her at all;
You go on to mass –
Won't we look after her.'

Flying

Mary's mind rises up above her body,
Looks down on the birthing scene below,
Her mother wiping her face gently
With a soft green towel that Kate sent
From New York as a wedding present;
The sheets rucked up above her waist,
Her hair sprawling on the pillow,
The midlife Mrs Gannon peering close,
Mouthing something; she thinks she sees
The word 'pain', then hears it,
The voice saying 'one more good pain.'
She laughs and tries to say 'there is no pain,
I'm not there at all, I'm here, look up ...'
She floats in over the kitchen, sees John
By the fire sharpening scallops for a creel,
Never idle, he pauses, knife mid-air, listens
For sounds from the room – a cry, a call.
Outside, the byre needs new thatch, the dunkle
should be moved further from the house but
that won't be easy. The apple trees are rich
this year, red currants and white currants galore,
the haggard is ready for the meitheal, a base
of alder branches set to build the rick of hay.

This thirteen acres is a world, she floats above it,
The meadows shorn, the harvest of grass in cones
Of serene beauty – yes beauty, she decides –
Even the cross black short-horn cow is beautiful,
Though she'll kick again first chance she gets;
The baby, she knows, will be a boy,
They'll name him Hugh –
for the Hugh who left here for America
and for John's father.
Now, says her mother's voice, now.
One last good push, the hair is black, a boy.

Asylum

She'll find the art of flying useful later
When she's strapped down for ECT,
Her struggles useless against the strength
Of three nurses or attendants,
She can never tell the difference.
And so she soars out over the grey walls
And drinks in the yellow of the daffodils,
Watches the men and women pottering
In the garden – once she counted forty
And she was sure Rose Wynne was one.
If she can hold for long enough
She'll see the lake and drift of swans
But then the blazing blast of light
Like she's hit the sun, or it's hit her.
She falls and falls, drops swiftsteep
Into what she'll later call oblivion.

ENDA WYLEY

Ghost

Who only wants
to come in –
who waits in the rain
in the yard,
who huddles
by the back door,
leaning into
the empty
wine bottles,
the damp leaves
and cobwebs,
who watches
the bamboo heavy
with snow shake
in the cold wind.
The neighbour's lights
go out, the door locks
and you,
who only wants
to come in,
enters through
my dreams.

You who were
kind in life
are kind now,
still with your own
particular ways –
your pale skin,

how you suck
your lower lip
and how you stare.
You come in
with a message
but first I need to ask,
And are you really dead?
When you nod
I know
you have come
to ask for a memory
of what you did
while here –
little girl dancing
to the Beatles
in your mother's
silver party dress,
little girl waltzing
with your best friend,
breathless,
your cheeks red.
Little girl, who wants only
not to forget.

NOTES ON CONTRIBUTORS

Alex Barclay is the author of four novels: *Darkhouse* and *The Caller* featuring NYPD Detective Joe Lucchesi, and *Blood Runs Cold* and *Time of Death* with FBI Special Agent Ren Bryce. The sequel to *Time of Death* will be out in early 2012. **Leland Bardwell** is among the senior figures in Irish writing. A poet, playwright, memoirist and novelist, she is a member of Aosdána. Among her most recent publications are *A Restless Life* (Liberties Press, 2008) and reissues of a number of her early novels from Blackstaff Press. **Kevin Barry** is the author of the story collection, *There Are Little Kingdoms,* and the novel, *City of Bohane.* His stories have appeared in the *New Yorker,* the *Granta Book of the Irish Short Story, Best European Fiction 2011,* and many other journals and anthologies. He lives in Co. Sligo. **Sara Berkeley** grew up in Ireland and now lives in the San Francisco Bay Area. She has had five collections of poetry published, most recently *The View from Here* (Gallery Press, 2010); also a collection of short stories *The Swimmer in the Deep Blue Dream* (Raven/Thistledown, 1992) and a novel *Shadowing Hannah* (New Island Books, 1999). Her poetry has been nominated for a Pushcart Prize. **Dermot Bolger** is a poet, fiction writer, playwright and editor, whose many awards include the Irish Times/ESB Irish Theatre Award for best new play in 2004 for *From These Green Heights.* He has published nine novels including *The Family on Paradise Pier* (2005) and his poems are collected as *Taking My Letters Back - New & Selected Poems* (1998). He is a member of Aosdána. **Pat Boran** is a poet, fiction writer, broadcaster and publisher. His publications include *New and Selected Poems* (2007), the memoir *The Invisible Prison* (2009), and the popular writers' handbook *The Portable Creative Writing Workshop.* A member of Aosdána, he received the 2008 Lawrence O'Shaughnessy Award for Poetry. **Colm Breathnach** was born in Cork. He has published six collections of poetry. His selected poems *Rogha Dánta 1991–2006* appeared in 2008. A novel *Con Trick "An Bhalla Bháin"* was published in 2009. In 1999 the Irish American Cultural Institute presented him with the Butler Award for his poetry. **Paddy Bushe** was born in Dublin and now lives in Co. Kerry. Among his eight poetry publications, in English and Irish, are *To Ring in Silence: New and Selected Poems* (Dedalus Press, 2008) and, as editor, *Voices at the World's Edge: Irish Poets on Skellig Michael* (Dedalus, 2010). His new collection is due in 2012. He is a member of Aosdána. **Philip Casey** lives in Dublin. He has published four volumes of poetry, the most recent of which is *Dialogue in Fading Light.* Also a novelist, he is a member of Aosdána. **Harry Clifton** was born in Dublin where he has recently resettled after many years abroad. He has published five collections of poetry in Ireland and the UK, as well as *Secular Eden: Paris*

Notebooks 1994-2004 in the US in 2007. He is the Ireland Professor of Poetry and a member of Aosdána. **Michael Coady** lives in his birthplace, Carrick-on-Suir. A writer of poetry and prose and also a photographer and musician, he is a member of Aosdána and has received a number of literary awards at home and abroad. He has had five books published by Gallery Press, the most recent being *Going by Water* (2009), which integrates poetry, short prose and photographs in an orchestrated genre he has made his own. **Evelyn Conlon** was born in Monaghan and lives in Rathmines, Dublin. She has published three novels, including *Skin of Dreams,* three collections of stories, including *Taking Scarlet as a Real Colour,* which has just been translated into Tamil, and edited four books, including *Later On: The Monaghan Bombing Memorial Book.* She is a member of Aosdána. **Susan Connolly** lives in Drogheda, Co. Louth. Her first collection of poetry, *For the Stranger,* was published by the Dedalus Press in 1993, and it is from it that the poem included here is taken. She was awarded the Patrick and Katherine Kavanagh Fellowship in Poetry in 2001. Her second collection, *Forest Music,* was published by Shearsman Books in 2009. **Enda Coyle-Greene** lives in Co. Dublin. Her first collection, *Snow Negatives,* won the Patrick Kavanagh Award in 2006 and was published in 2007 by the Dedalus Press. In 2009 she received an MA in English – Creative Writing, with Distinction, from the Seamus Heaney Centre for Poetry at Queen's University, Belfast. **Tony Curtis** was born in Dublin in 1955. He is the author of seven warmly received collections, most recently *Folk* (Arc Publications, 2011). He has been awarded the Irish National Poetry Prize and is a member of Aosdána. **Pádraig J Daly** was born in Dungarvan, Co. Waterford and lives in Ballyboden, Dublin where he works as an Augustinian priest. He has published numerous collections of poetry, most recently *Afterlife* (2010) and *Clinging to the Myth* (2007) and translates from the Irish and the Italian. **Philip Davison** has published seven novels, among them, *The Crooked Man, McKenzie's Friend, The Long Suit* and *A Burnable Town.* He writes for stage and radio. His most recent play is *Love and Animals.* **Gerald Dawe** was born in Belfast and lives in Dun Laoghaire. He has published seven collections of poetry, most recently *Points West* (2008). *Conversations: Poets & Poetry* is published in 2011, to be followed in 2012 by *Selected Poems.* He is a fellow of Trinity College Dublin. **John F Deane** was born on Achill Island. A poet, novelist and short storywriter, he was the Founder of Poetry Ireland and of the Poetry Ireland Review. His most recently poetry volume is *Eye of the Hare* (Carcanet, 2011). He was recently awarded the highest Serbian prize for literature, The Golden Key of Smederevo, to include a collection of his poems published in dual-language format in Belgrade this year. **Patrick Deeley** was born in Loughrea, Co. Galway, and lives in Dublin. He has published five collections of poetry with the Dedalus Press, the most recent of which is *The Bones of Creation*. His novel for children, *The Lost Orchard*, won the 2001 Eilis Dillon Memorial Award. **Greg Delanty** was born in Cork and is a long-time US resident. His latest books are *Collected Poems, 1986–2006* (Carcanet Press), *The New Citizen Army* (Combat Paper Project) and *The Word Exchange: Anglo-Saxon Poems in Translation* (WW Norton). **Theo Dorgan** was born in Cork and lives in Dublin. Hs most recent books are *Time On The Ocean*, a prose account of a South Atlantic journey under sail, and *Greek* (Dedalus Press), a collection of poems. Both books appeared in 2010, when he was recipient of The Lawrence O'Shaughnessy Award for Irish Poetry (USA). He is a member of Aosdána. **Paul Durcan** (b. 1944) is one of Ireland's best-known poets. His many collections include *Daddy, Daddy* (1990), which won the Whitbread Poetry Prize, *Crazy About Women* (1991), *Greetings to Our Friends in Brazil* (1999) and *The Art of Life* (2004). *Paul Durcan's Diary*, a compilation of his radio broadcasts was published in 2003 and *Life is a Dream: 40 years of Reading Poems*, 1967–2007, was published by Harvill Secker in 2009 2009. 'Thinking About Suicide' will be included in his new book in 2012. He is a member of Aosdána. **Christine Dwyer Hickey** is a novelist and short-story writer. Her novel *Tatty* was short-listed for Irish Book of the Year in 2005 and was also long-listed for The Orange Prize. Her novels, *The Dancer*, *The Gambler* and *The Gatemaker* were re-issued in 2006 as *The Dublin Trilogy*. She was also a prize winner in the Observer/Penguin short-story competition. Her latest novel is *Last Train from Liguria* (2009). She is a member of Aosdána. **Peter Fallon** is founder, editor and publisher of The Gallery Press (1970 -). His books include *News of the World: Selected and New Poems*, *The Georgics of Virgil* (Oxford World Classics) and *The Company of Horses*. A member of Aosdána and Adjunct Professor of English at Trinity College, Dublin, he lives in Loughcrew in County Meath where he farmed for many years. **Gerard Fanning** was born in Dublin in 1952. He was educated at University College Dublin. His latest collection is *Hombre: New & Selected Poems* (Dedalus, 2011). **Gabriel Fitzmauric**e was born, in 1952, in the village of Moyvane, Co. Kerry where he still lives. He is author of more than forty books, including collections of poetry in English and Irish as well as several collections of verse for children. He has translated extensively from the Irish and has edited a number of anthologies of poetry in English and Irish. He has published two volumes of essays and collections of songs and ballads. His latest book is *Poems of Faith and Doubt* from Salmon Poetry. **Miriam Gamble** is from Belfast but now lives in Glasgow. Her debut collection, *The Squirrels are Dead*, is published by Bloodaxe Books. She works as a subtitler for the hard of hearing. Boston-born **Anthony Glavin** lives in Dublin where he works as a books editor, writer and critic. Author of a critically acclaimed novel *Nighthawk Alley*, he has also published two short story collections, *One for Sorrow* and *The Draughtsman and The Unicorn*. **Eamon Grennan** was born in Dublin in 1941 and educated at UCD, where he studied English and Italian, and Harvard, where he received his PhD in English. His collections of poetry from The Gallery Press include *What Light There Is* (1987), *So It Goes* (1995), *Selected and New Poems* (2000), *The Quick of It* (2004) and *Out of Breath* (2007). Other publications include *Leopardi: Selected Poems* (Dedalus, 1995) and *Facing the Music* (1999), a collection of essays on modern Irish poetry. **Vona Groarke** was born in 1964. She has published five collection of poems with the Gallery Press, among them *Flight* (2002), shortlisted for the Forward Prize (UK) in 2002 and winner of the Michael Hartnett Award in 2003, *Juniper Street* (2006) and *Spindrift* (2009), a Poetry Book Society Recommendation. Awards include the Hennessy Award, the Brendan Behan Memorial Prize, Strokestown International Poetry Award, and the Stand Magazine Poetry Prize. She teaches in the Centre for New Writing at the University of Manchester. **Kerry Hardie** was born in 1951 and lives in Co. Kilkenny. She has published five collections of poetry with the Gallery Press, the most recent of which is *Only This Room*. She has also written two novels [Harper Collins], and Gallery Press / Bloodaxe have recently published a *Selected Poems*. Awards include a Katherine and Patrick Kavanagh Fellowship, the Michael Hartnett Award. and the Lawrence O'Shaughnessy Award (USA). **James Harpur** was born in the UK in 1956 and now lives in Co. Cork. His four poetry collections are published by Anvil Press including *The Dark Age* (2007), which won the 2009 Michael Hartnett Award. Other prizes and bursaries include the 1995 British National Poetry Competition, two Arts Council of Ireland Bursaries, a Society of Authors Bursary, an Eric Gregory Award, and a Hawthornden Fellowship. **Jack Harte**'s most recent book is *Unravelling the Spiral* (Scotus Press, 2010), a memoir/biography of the sculptor Fred Conlon. His fiction includes the collection of stories *From Under Gogol's Nose* and the novels *In the Wake of the Bagger* and *Reflections in a Tar-Barrel*, an extract of which is included here. He is currently Chairman of the Irish Writers' Centre. **Dermot Healy** was born Co. Westmeath in 1947. His most recent novel *Long Time, No See* was published by Faber and Faber in 2011, and his most recent book of poems *A Fool's Errand* was published by Gallery Press in 2010. He lives in Co. Sligo, and is a member of Aosdána. **Michael D Higgins** was born in Limerick in 1941 and raised in Co. Clare. In 1992, he became the first recipient of the Seán McBride International Peace Medal for his work for human rights. He is a Labour TD for Galway West and has twice been Mayor of Galway. He has published three collections of poems, most recently *An Arid Season: New Poems* (2004). *New and Selected Poems* appeared in 2011 from Liberties Press. **Rita Ann Higgins** has published eight collections of poetry. Five with

Salmon publishing and three with Bloodaxe, including *Throw in the Vowels: New and Selected Poems* (2005, reissued in 2010 with audio CD). In 2010 Salmon published *Hurting God (part essay, part rhyme)*. Forthcoming from Bloodaxe in Autumn 2011 is a new collection of poetry called *Ireland is Changing Mother.* **Fred Johnston** was born in Belfast in 1951 and has lived for many years in Galway. He has published several collections of poetry and four novels. In 1986 he founded the annual Cúirt literature festival in Galway. **Claire Keegan** was born in 1968 and grew up on a farm in Wicklow. Her debut collection of stories, *Antarctica*, appeared to universal acclaim in 1999 and was followed in 2007 by *Walk the Blue Fields*. Her 'long, short story' *Foster* was published in 2010. Her many awards include the William Trevor Prize, the Rooney Prize for Irish Literature, the Olive Cook Award and the Davy Byrnes Irish Writing Award 2009 and two Francis MacManus Awards. **Brendan Kennelly** is one of Ireland's best known and most popular poets, whose many collections include *Cromwell* (1983), *The Book of Judas,* (1991), *Poetry Me Arse* (1995), *The Man Made of Rain* (1998) and *Reservoir Voices* (2009). **Thomas Kinsella** was born in Dublin in 1928 and now lives in Philadelphia. One of the senior figures in Irish writing, he is the author of over thirty collections of poetry, has translated extensively from the Irish, notably the epic *The Táin,* and edited *The New Oxford Book of Irish Verse,* among other volumes. He was a director of the Dolmen Press and Cuala Press, and in 1972 founded Peppercanister Press, in recent times facilitated by Dedalus. Carcanet published *Collected Poems* in 2001. He received the Freedom of the City of Dublin in 2007. **Anatoly Kudryavitsky** is a Russian/Irish poet and novelist living in Co. Dublin. He has published two novels and ten collections of poetry, three of them in English; the latest being *Capering Moons* (Doghouse Books, 2011). *A Night in the Nabokov Hotel,* his anthology of contemporary Russian poetry in English translation, was published by Dedalus Press in 2006. **Jessie Lendennie** is co-founder and Managing Director of Salmon Poetry Ltd, established in 1981. Her poetry collections are *Daughter and Other Poems* (2002) and *Walking Here* (2011). She has edited several anthologies, including *Dogs Singing: A Tribute Anthology* and *Poetry: Reading It, Writing It, Publishing It.* Dundalk-born **Jinx Lennon** is a poet / troubadour. His latest album is *National Cancer Strategy. www.jinxlennon.com.* **Dave Lordan** has published two collections of poems, the most recent being *Invitation to a Sacrifice* (Salmon Poetry, 2010). Forthcoming are the *First Book of Frags* from Wurm Press in Nov 2011 and his first collection of short stories, *Out of My Head,* due from Salmon in Summer 2012. **Aifric Mac Aodha** is the literary editor of the Irish language magazine *Comhar* and Irish language poetry editor of the Stinging Fly. She works as a translator for the New English-Irish Dictionary and lectures in University College Dublin. Her translator Ian Ó Caoimh is the editor of

Comhar. He works as a translator in the Houses of the Oireachtas and is preparing a Ph.D. on Ciarán Ó Nualláin. **Catherine Phil MacCarthy** grew up in Co. Limerick and lives in Dublin. Collections include *This Hour of the Tide,* Salmon Publishing (1994); *the blue globe* (1998), *Suntrap,* (2007), and a first novel, *One Room an Everywhere* (2003), published by Blackstaff Press. She is winner of *The Fish Poetry Prize,* Bantry 2010, and a former editor of *Poetry Ireland Review.* **John MacKenna** is the author of sixteen books. His most recent novel is *The Space Between Us* (New Island Books, 2009). His new collection of short stories and a volume of poems are due for publication in 2012. He is a winner of the Hennessy, Cecil Day Lewis and Irish Times Fiction Awards. **Tom Mathews** is one of Ireland's best-known cartoonists, contributing to a wide range of newspapers and periodicals and illustrating more than a dozen books. He has published three volumes of his cartoons and a novel, and his first collection of poems, *The Owl and the Pussycat and other poems,* was published by Dedalus in 2009. **Joan McBreen** was born in Sligo and now divides her time between Tuam and Renvyle County Galway. She has published four collections of poetry, the most recent of which is *Heather Island,* (2009). She is also the editor of two anthologies *The White Page/ An Bhileog Bhán: Twentieth-Century Irish Women Poets,* and *The Watchful Heart: A New Generation of Irish Poets— Poems and Essays.* **Colum McCann** was born in Dublin and currently lives in New York. He is the author of five novels and two collections of stories, published in some 30 languages. His novel *Let the Great World Spin* has been a bestseller on four continents and has won many prizes, among them the 2011 IMPAC International Prize and, in China, the 21st Century Best Foreign Novel of the Year award. H is movie *Everything In This Country Must* was nominated for a short-film Oscar in 2005. **Molly McCloskey** was born in Philadelphia and has lived in Ireland since 1989. She is the author of two collections of short stories and a novel. *In Circles Around the Sun* (Penguin Ireland, 2011). her first work of non-fiction, she pieces together her brother's life before and after he began to suffer from schizophrenia, and explores the effects of the illness on Mike and on other members of the family. **Mike McCormack** was born in Sligo in 1965. His stories are collected as *Getting it in the Head* (1998), for which he won the Rooney Prize. His novels are *Crowe's Requiem* (1999); and *Notes from a Coma* (2005), all from Jonathan Cape. **Hugh McFadden** is a poet, critic, and literary editor. Born in Derry, he lives in Dublin. He is the author of three collections of poetry, the most recent being *Elegies & Epiphanies* (Lagan Press, Belfast, 2005). He is the executor of the literary estate of John Jordan, and recently edited *John Jordan: Selected Poems* (Dedalus Press, Dublin, 2008). **Iggy McGovern** was born in Coleraine and now lives in Dublin. He has published two collections of poetry with Dedalus Press, the most recent of which is *Safe House* (2010).

He is the recipient of the Glen Dimplex New Writers Award for Poetry 2000. **Máighréad Medbh** was born in Newcastle West, Co. Limerick, and now lives in Swords, Co. Dublin. She has published five collections of poems, the most recent of which is *Twelve Beds for the Dreamer* (Arlen House, 2010). She has also produced a CD, *Out of My Skin. www.maighreadmedbh.ie.* **Paula Meehan**, poet and playwright, was born in Dublin where she still lives. Her most recent collections of poetry are *Dharmakaya* (2000, which received the Denis Devlin Award for Poetry) and *Painting Rain* (2009) They are both available from Carcanet Press in the UK and Wake Forest University Press in the USA. **Lia Mills** writes novels, short stories and essays. Her most recent book, *In Your Face* (Penguin Ireland, 2007), is a memoir of her experience of mouth cancer. She is currently working on her third novel. **Judith Mok** was born in the Netherlands and lives in Ireland. She has has published three novels and three books of poetry. Her new book of poetry, *Gods of Babel*, appeared in September 2011. She travels the world working as a classical singer. **John Montague** was born in Brooklyn and educated in Northern Ireland, Dublin and the US. His major publications include *The Rough Field, The Great Cloak, The Dead Kingdom, Mount Eagle* and *Smashing the Piano*. *Collected Poems* appeared in 1995, the year he received the American Ireland Fund Literary Award. Other recent books include *Drunken Sailor* (2004), *In My Grandfather's Mansion* (2010) and *Speech Lessons* (2011), all from the Gallery Press. In 1998 he became the first Ireland Professor of Poetry, and in 2010 the French State honoured him as a Chevalier de la Légion d'Honneur. **Sinéad Morrissey** was born in 1972 and grew up in Belfast. Her four collections of poetry are *There Was Fire in Vancouver* (1996), *Between Here and There* (2002), *The State of the Prisons* (2005) and *Through the Square Window* (2009), all from Carcanet Press. She has lived in Germany, Japan and New Zealand and now lectures in creative writing at the Seamus Heaney Centre for Poetry, Queen's University, Belfast. **Paul Murray** is a Dominican priest, born in Newcastle, Co. Down and now living in Rome. In 1991 the Dedalus Press published his third collection of poems, *The Absent Fountain*, which was followed in 2003 by *These Black Stars*. **Nuala Ní Chonchúir** was born in Dublin and now lives in County Galway. She has published one novel, *You* (New Island, 2010), three short fiction collections, and three volumes of poetry; her third full poetry collection *The Juno Charm* is due from Salmon in late 2011. *www.nualanichonchuir.com.* **Eiléan Ní Chuilleanáin** was born in Cork city in 1942. She was a founder member of the literary journal *Cyphers*. Her collections of poetry include *Acts and Monuments* (1972), *The Second Voyage* (1977, 1986), *The Magdalene Sermon* (1989), shortlisted for the Irish Times/Aer Lingus Award, *The Girl Who Married the Reindeer* (2001) and *The Sun-fish* (2009), winner of the prestigious International Griffin Poetry Prize. She is a member of Aosdána.

Nuala Ní Dhomhnaill was born in 1952 and grew up in the Irish-speaking areas of West Kerry and in Tipperary. She has published four collections of poems in Irish, among them *Feis* (1991) and *Cead Aighnis* (1998), while the Gallery Press has published four collections, with translations into English, among them *Pharaoh's Daughter* (1990), *The Water Horse* (translations by Medbh McGuckian and Eiléan Ní Chuilleanáin, 1999) and *The Fifty Minute Mermaid* (translations by Paul Muldoon, 2007). She was Ireland Professor of Poetry (2002-2004) and is a member of Aosdána. **Jean O'Brien** was born in Dublin and lives in Co. Laois. Her most recent book of poems is *Lovely Legs* (2009). Her next collection, *Love Handles* will be published, also by Salmon Publishing, in Spring 2012. She teaches Creative Writing in the Irish Writers' Centre. She was the winner of the 2010 Arvon International Poetry Award. **Joseph O'Connor** was born in Dublin. He is the author of the novels *Cowboys and Indians Desperadoes, The Salesman, Inishowen, Star of the Sea* and *Redemption Falls,* as well as a number of bestselling works of non-fiction. A hugely popular broadcaster he has also written film scripts and stage-plays including the award-winning *Red Roses and Petrol.* His many awards include France's Prix Millepages, Italy's Premio Acerbi, the Irish Post Award for Fiction, the Neilsen Bookscan Golden Book Award, an American Library Association Award, the Hennessy / Sunday Tribune Hall of Fame Award, and the Prix Litteraire Zepter for European Novel of the Year. His most recent novel, *Ghost Light,* spent nine weeks as a number one Irish bestseller and was chosen as Dublin's *One City One Book* novel for 2011. **Mary O'Donoghue**'s most recent poetry collection is *Among These Winters* (Dedalus Press, 2007). Her debut novel *Before the House Burns* appeared from Lilliput Press in 2010. She lives in Boston, USA. **John O'Donnell** was born and lives in Dublin. He won the Hennessy / Sunday Tribune New Irish Writing Award for Poetry in 1998, and in 2001 The Ireland Fund's Listowel Writers' Week Prizes for Best Individual Poem and Best Short Collection. He has published two books of poems, most recently *Icarus Sees His Father Fly* (Dedalus, 2004). Poet and fiction writer **Mary O'Donnell** is the author of eleven books of poetry and fiction, including the best-selling novel *The Light-Makers, Virgin and the Boy,* and *The Elysium Testament,* as well as a number of poetry collections, most recently *The Ark Builders* (Arc Publications, 2009). Her essays on contemporary literary issues are widely published and she has presented a number of literary programs on RTÉ Radio 1. She is a member of Aosdána. **Dennis O'Driscoll**'s eight books of poetry include *New and Selected Poems* (Anvil Press, 2004), a Poetry Book Society Special Commendation, and *Reality Check* (Anvil Press, 2007), shortlisted for the Irish Times / Poetry Now Prize 2008. A selection of his essays and reviews, *Troubled Thoughts, Majestic Dreams* (Gallery Press), was published in 2001. He is editor of the *Bloodaxe Book of Poetry Quotations*

(2006). His book, *Stepping Stones: Interviews with Seamus Heaney* (Faber and Faber), was published in 2008. **Michael O'Loughlin** was born in Dublin in 1958 and lives in Ireland after many years abroad. His poetry collections include *Stalingrad: The Street Dictionary* (1980), *Atlantic Blues* (1982), *The Diary of a Silence* (1985), *Another Nation: New & Selected Poems* (1994) and *In This Life* (2011). His collection of short stories, *The Inside Story*, appeared in 1999 and his translation of Dutch poet Gerrit Achterberg's selected poems, *Hidden Weddings*, in 1987. *The Jewish Bride* is a fictionalised account of the life of the 17th century false messiah, Sabbatei Sevi. **Nessa O'Mahony** was born in Dublin and lives in Rathfarnham where she works as a freelance teacher and writer. She has published three books – her first collection, *Bar Talk*, appeared in 1999. Her second, *Trapping a Ghost*, was published in 2005. A verse novel, *In Sight of Home*, was published by Salmon in 2009. **Mary O'Malley** was born in Connemara and lives in the Moycullen Gaeltacht. Her many poetry collections include *The Knife in the Wave* (1997), *Asylum Road* (2001) and *The Boning Hall: New and Selected Poems* (2002). She is a member of Aosdána. **Liam Ó Muirthile** is from Cork. He is currently working on a new collection of poems as well as *New and Selected Poems/Rogha Dánta*. He is a member of Aosdána. **Micheal O'Siadhail** has published thirteen volumes of poetry, his latest being *Tongues* (Bloodaxe, 2010). Recipient of an Irish American Cultural Institute prize for poetry and the Marten Toonder Prize for Literature, he has read and broadcast his poetry in Ireland, Britain, Europe, North America and Japan. **Leanne O'Sullivan** was born in 1983 and comes from the Beara Peninsula, Co. Cork. Her most recent collection, *Cailleach: The Hag of Beara* was published by Bloodaxe Books in 2009. **Maeve O'Sullivan** was born in Dublin. She has published her poems and haiku widely, and is a former poetry winner at Listowel Writer's Week. She is a member of Haiku Ireland, the Poetry Divas and the Hibernian Poetry Workshop. Her first haiku collection, *Initial Response*, was published in spring 2011 by Alba Publishing. **Paul Perry** has published three collections of poems, the most recent of which is *The Last Falcon and Small Ordinance* (Dedalus Press, 2010). He has held a number of Writer-in-Residence positions and currently directs the Faber Academy's 'Becoming a Poet' writing course in Dublin. **Billy Ramsell** was born in Cork where he still lives. His debut collection of poems, *Complicated Pleasures*, appeared from Dedalus in 2007. **Maurice Riordan** was born in Lisgoold, Co. Cork, and now lives in London. He has published three collections of poems with Faber. The most recent, *The Holy Land* (2007), received the Michael Hartnett Award. **Mark Roper** has published five poetry collections, most recently *Even So: New & Selected Poems* (Dedalus Press, 2008). *The River Book,* a collaboration with photographer Paddy Dwan, was published in 2010. A new poetry collection, *Keeping Distance,* is due from Dedalus in

2012. **Gabriel Rosenstock** is an Irish poet, haiku writer, translator and author, primarily in the Irish language, with more than a 100 books to his credit. Born in Kilfinane, Co. Limerick in 1949 he lives in Dublin. Dedalus published the bilingual *Bliain an Bhandé / Year of the Goddess* in 2007. He is a member of Aosdána. **Peter Sheridan** was born in Dublin in 1952 and is a playwright, screenwriter and director. He wrote and directed the film *Borstal Boy,* based upon Brendan Behan's memoir and is the author of the best-selling *44: A Dublin Memoir* (PanMacmillan, 1999) as well as *Forty-Seven Roses* (2001). **Gerard Smyth** was born and lives in Dublin where, until recently, he worked in journalism for many years. He is the author of six poetry collections, most recently *The Mirror Tent* (2007) and *The Fullness of Time: New and Selected Poems* (Dedalus Press, 2010). **Peter Sirr** lives in Dublin where he works as a freelance writer and translator. His most recent collection of poems is *The Thing Is* (Gallery Press, 2009), which won the 2011 Michael Hartnett Award. He is a member of Aosdána. **Richard Tillinghast** is an American poet with long connections to Ireland. He is the author of ten books of poetry, most recently *The New Life,* 2008, and *Selected Poems (Dedalus Press,* 2009), as well as *Dirty August,* translations from the Turkish poet, Edip Cansever, also 2009. **Colm Tóibín** was born in Enniscorthy, Co. Wexford in 1955. He has won numerous awards for his writing, including the Whitbread First Novel Award for *The South,* the Encore Award for *The Heather Blazing* (1992), the Dublin IMPAC Prize and the LA Times Novel of the Year for *The Master* (2004) and the Costa Novel of the Year Award for *Brooklyn* (2009). He edited *The Penguin Book of Irish Fiction,* and *The Modern Library: the 200 Best Novels since 1950* (with Carmen Callil), while his non-fiction includes *The Sign of the Cross: Travels in Catholic Europe* (1994). He is currently Leonard Milberg Lecturer in Irish Letters at Princeton University. **Eamonn Wall** was born in Co. Wexford and now lives in St. Louis, Missouri, USA. His most recent publications are *Writing the Irish West* (University of Notre Dame Press), a book of criticism, and *Sailing Lake Mareotis* (Salmon), a collection of poetry, both appearing in 2011. **Grace Wells** was born in London and lives in Co. Tipperary. Her first book, *Gyrfalcon* (2002), a novel for children, won the Eilis Dillon Best Newcomer Bisto Award, and was an International White Ravens' Choice. Other publications for children include *Ice-Dreams* (2008) and *One World, Our World* (2009). Her debut collection of poems, *When God Has Been Called Away to Greater Things* was published by Dedalus in 2010. **David Wheatley** was born in Dublin in 1970 and lives in Hull. He has published four books with Gallery Press, the most recent of which is *A Nest on the Waves* (2010). **Macdara Woods** was born in Dublin in 1945. His poetry collections include *Selected Poems* (1996), *The Nightingale Water* and *Knowledge in the Blood* (2002), Artichoke Wine (2006) and *The Cotard Dimension* (2011).

His work has been translated widely, into some 12 languages set to music by artists such as Anuna and Bonita Hill. He is a member of Aosdána. In 2012 Dedalus Press will issue his *Collected Poems*. **Vincent Woods** was born in Co. Leitrim in 1960. Plays include *At the Black Pig's Dyke* (1992), *Song of the Yellow Bittern* (1994), both with Druid and *A Cry From Heaven* (Abbey Theatre, 2005. Poetry collections are *The Colour of Language* (1994) and *Lives and Miracles*, with drawings by Charles Cullen (Arlen House, 2006). Awards include The Stewart Parker Award for Drama, 1993, the PJ O'Connor Award for Radio Drama, and the M.J. McManus Award for Poetry. He is a member of Aosdána and host of 'Arts Tonight' on RTÉ Radio 1. **Enda Wyley** was born and lives in Dublin. The most recent of her four poetry collections from the Dedalus Press is *To Wake To This* (2009). She is a teacher in Dublin's inner city and also writes for children, *The Silver Notebook* (2007) and *I Won't Go to China!* (2009) being her most recent publications for younger readers.

Dedalus Press
New Writing from Ireland and the World

Established in 1985, the Dedalus Press is one of Ireland's best-known literary imprints, with a particular interest in new Irish poetry.

For further information on Dedalus Press titles, including links to our AudioRoom podcast, visit **www.dedaluspress.com**.

"One of the most outward-looking poetry presses in Ireland and the UK"
—UNESCO.org

Supporting People Affected by Mental Ill Health

By purchasing this book you have assisted Shine in raising awareness of our organisation and mental health issues.

Shine is the national organisation dedicated to upholding the rights and addressing the needs of all those affected by mental ill health, through the promotion and provision of high quality services and through working to ensure the continual enhancement of the quality of life of the people it serves.

Shine believes that people with mental ill health should at all times be accorded equal rights, entitlements and opportunities available to any other member of society, and should be empowered to participate in the life of the community. Family members, the majority of whom are the primary providers of mental healthcare in the community, should be accorded full recognition and support by the institutions of the State, and be empowered to address their own needs. A history of mental ill health should not be a cause for discrimination in any form, nor should it inhibit the individual's right of equal access to training, education and employment/opportunities. Shine fosters a partnership approach with all relevant agencies to support people with mental health problems.

Shine supports people with mental health problems and their families in a number of different ways through our information helpline, our regional development offices, our resource centres based in Dublin and Cork and counselling services which are also provided in Dublin and Cork.

Our confidential information helpline 1890 621 631 is open Monday to Friday from 9 am to 4 pm and can provide general information, a listening ear and specific information about Shine's services. For more information on Shine please visit our website **www.shineonline.ie**